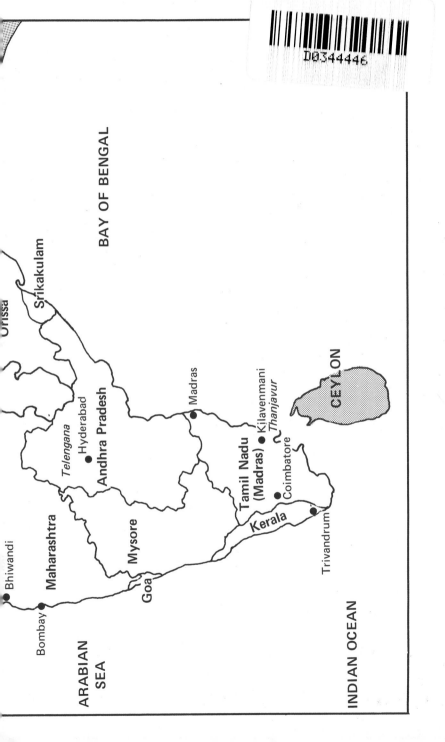

ARABIAN
SEA

Bhiwandi

Bombay

Maharashtra

Goa

Mysore

Telengana

Hyderabad

Andhra Pradesh

Orissa

Srikakulam

BAY OF BENGAL

Madras

Tamil Nadu
(Madras)

Kilavenmani

Thanjavur

Coimbatore

Kerala

Trivandrum

CEYLON

INDIAN OCEAN

FACE TO FACE
fascism and revolution in India

English translation by Norman Kurtin
Lasse and Lisa Berg

Ramparts Press
Berkeley, California

Contents

COMMUNISM AND REVOLUTION

Lasse and Lisa Berg, two young Swedish journalists, visited India in 1966 as tourists, and then returned in 1968-69 to do sociological research on revolutionary peasant movements. In the course of their second visit they traveled widely in the Indian countryside and spent much of their time living in villages; this book is the outcome of that experience.

FACE TO FACE was originally published in Swedish, part of it as articles in the newspaper *Dagens Nyheter*. This edition has been brought up to date and revised for American readers.   —*The Editors*

THE
VILLAGES

conversations
in Makhaupur

North India in December. We are visiting a village, a completely ordinary Indian village, one of the five hundred thousand villages in this country. This one is called Makhaupur and is just outside Allahabad in the eastern portion, the poorest section, of Uttar Pradesh. No one really knows how old the village is. No one really knows how old he is himself. It is quiet—to us surprisingly quiet. In some way the Western "birth control image" of India is in the back of our minds—the image of India as one big crowd, people everywhere.

But in the villages—seen from outside—silence reigns.

We go through the village. We're the first foreigners to visit the village and everyone collects around us, looks at us, follows us. We go first through the quarter of the casteless, on the small paths between the earth huts. Everything is the same color, the same light sandy color—the earth, the houses. Some of the houses have fallen apart during the monsoon. The only colorful things we see are the women's clothes—saris in radiant red, gold, blue, green. Women and children sit outside their small houses; they sit quiet and unmoving. The children are naked or wear dirty rags; they have big swollen stomachs and their faces are covered with flies around their eyes and mouths. Some goats and cows munch at the few blades of grass the dry earth supports.

We pass by the well of the casteless where some women are drawing water in a leather skin and emptying it into tin containers to carry home skillfully balanced on their proud, erect heads.

Next to the casteless section is the low-caste section— slightly sturdier houses, but also built of earth. Simple plows hang on the walls, plows to be drawn by oxen. On one wall we see, written in Hindi, "A small family is a happy family" —a vestige of the visit of the family planning information officer to the village. Someone has painted little red flowers around the entrance to his house. There are no doors and windows, only a hole for the entrance. Food is prepared on an open fire outside. In this village, one sleeps on the earth floor if one is poor, on a rope bed if one is rich.

We pass by the low-caste well. Two oxen pull the line attached to the water-skin; just now the creaking noise of the line is the only thing to be heard in the whole village.

Then we come to the high-caste section, brick buildings or white-painted stone houses with small flowers outside, dusty red hibiscus. Water buffalo and small casteless children bathe in a big, miry puddle in front of the houses. The high-caste children sit quietly in well-made cotton clothing and look at us.

Out in the fields there is no one—it is not the work season. Five or six months of the year there is no work in the fields; the villagers have nothing to do. Some perhaps are lucky and can find work as cycle rickshaw drivers in a large village or city nearby, and earn up to twenty cents a day, but this is rare; it's difficult to find jobs—most of the people sit in the village with nothing to do. Rice and wheat are growing in the fields—poorly. There is too little rain this year.

The two hundred families have only seven hundred acres

of land among them and its distribution is very lopsided. Three of the families, three brothers, own half the land—the best land. Many families are completely without land. The great majority of landowners have all too little, usually only a few acres. The result is that most live near the subsistence minimum and do not manage to work effectively. Gradually, they get in debt to the moneylender; once in debt they stay dependent, which makes changes difficult. The peasants also depend on the large landowners for occasional work to stretch their tiny incomes. Despite this the peasants and land-less in this district have recently begun to stand up and demand a more equitable division of the land. Some have even occupied the land. But this movement has not yet reached Makhaupur.

The men collect around us, sit in a ring with us, laugh and smile at us. The women do not; they stay at home—anything else would be unthinkable here. We talk with the men, ask a little about their everyday life. We listen to their answers.

Ramhid

"I am a *kamar*, a leatherworker. I am casteless. I take dead animals and skin them, and make things from them. We *kamar*s live together; we have our houses next to one another. Each caste lives separately. I own no land and no animals. I am a poor man. I get twenty cents a day for my work. My wife works too, in the fields, but she earns even less. We have two children. We have too little to eat. We eat mostly grain, sometimes we can get rice or wheat. It's a pity about my children. Two years ago, when we were starving, two children in the village died because they couldn't get any food. I'm afraid, sometimes think that next time the famine comes perhaps my children will die.

"I've lived here in this village all my life. My father and my grandfather lived here too. Everything here has been the same all my life. Nothing has changed, I can't think of a thing that has changed. People are born and die but everything's the same. We marry within the caste, we live with our caste, and my son will live as I live.

"If I could wish for something for our village it would be electricity. In the neighboring village, about a mile from here, there is electricity. With electricity we could have a water pump and irrigate. Then we could get better harvests; everyone would live better. I'd also like it if we had a small factory in the village where we could work when we weren't working in the fields, where we could earn a little money for food and clothes.

"If I could wish for land, I'd want to have four acres; it would be enough and I would be able to tend it. But I have no land. Take land? That I can't do; land reforms and such, only the great leaders can manage that, we can't do anything. The police would punish us. I don't know much about politics. I know about the government—the Congress party—and the communists, because they usually come to the village.

"I don't know much. I've never gone to school, can't read and write. I'm only a simple person."

Changalal

"I'm a farmworker, belonging to the *Ark* caste, a low caste. I own one acre of land. It's not enough. I'd like to have four acres. We have wheat and rice four months of the year, the rest of the year we have only grits. It's not good food. I earn one rupee* a day at most. It's not enough. I borrow money. I've borrowed more than two hundred dollars from the rich

* Fourteen cents.

man in the village for food and clothing for my family. Every year I must pay 75 percent interest on the loan. I must borrow money to pay the interest. My debts grow all the time, I don't know how I can ever get rid of them. I can't borrow money from the bank in the city because you must repay them so quickly—how could I do that?

"I don't like the rich. They make it impossible for us to live better. It's not fair that some people have a lot and others nothing at all. But what can we do about it? If we fight, the police will come.

"It's hard to say how poverty will be taken care of . . . I don't know how it will go. I'd like the government to give us a pump so we could irrigate. I wish we could get a better kind of grain so we'd have better harvests.

"I've lived in this village all my life, like my father and his father before him. I haven't noticed any change during my lifetime. Yes, there are more of us in the village; the village grows, but we don't get more food. We've become poorer. I don't know what will happen to me after I die. It depends on what God thinks about me. I believe in heaven, I think it's better there than here. It must be better in heaven than here. When the famine came two years ago we had nothing at all to eat for five days. I don't think such things happen in heaven."

Ram Vishal

"I belong to the *Wadev* caste, the dairyworkers. I own two bulls and three and a half acres of land which must support ten people, and it's quite impossible. There's not enough food.

"One day I realized we just couldn't live this way any longer, we just couldn't continue like this, we had to do something to improve things, to get more food, etc. I decided to borrow money for a pump; I borrowed $1,650 from the government, I thought that with the help of the pump we would be able to double the crop and improve things a lot and be able to pay back the money to the government gradually. I don't know anymore if it will work. The government takes 9.5 percent in interest. Even if my crop is doubled and we don't eat any more than now and save money for payments, it will still take ten years before I've repaid the debt. But we can't continue to live as we're living now, we're getting sick, my children are getting sick.

"There's one thing I want for my children: that they go to school. I shall try to get them into school in the neighboring village. We *Wadevs* may go to school, but the low castes, the Untouchables, may not. The teacher in the school won't take them. It's the same thing in all the villages around here. The poorest people in this village don't have enough money to let their children go to school anyway; they need their help in the fields and for other work. There are only twenty boys from our village who go to school now. Girls don't go to school at all.

"It's always been the same in this village as long as I can remember. Nothing has gotten better. I think that if the children could go to school things would get better. Maybe."

the green revolution
in Thanjavur

Kilavenmani

"Kilavenmani is a village here in Thanjavur, near the sea. A majority of the inhabitants are casteless farmworkers. They own no land, so they are dependent on the landowners who live in the neighboring villages. In the part of the village where it happened, fifty families lived—all farmworkers. Thirty-two huts. It happened at night."

We are sitting in one of those drab little brown rooms that fill India's cities. Peeling paint on the walls, rickety wood furniture, a portrait of Tagore* on the wall. Tea with buffalo milk and biscuits is on the table between us. We listen to a man's embittered voice; he speaks slowly, makes long pauses, listens to himself. His name is A. M. Govindarajan and he belongs to an investigation commission appointed to study the Kilavenmani murders.

"The landowners came and burned twenty-eight of the houses to the ground. They locked up forty-four casteless, mostly women and children, in one hut. They frightened them and drove them into the hut where they locked them in. Then they set fire to the building—a small hut.

* Rabindranath Tagore, the best-known modern Indian poet.

"We got there in the morning and saw all the burned bodies. We came at three o'clock in the morning. All the bodies were there, burnt to ashes. The hut was less than three yards square and perhaps one yard high. There lay all the bodies, forty-four bodies. They were destroyed by the fire, unrecognizable, it was not easy to make out people's faces, see whether they were men or women, everything was burnt away.

"Fourteen were women. They were from twelve to twenty-four years old. There were only three men, all the others were children. Words can't describe the atrocity. One woman named Papama had her one-year-old child clutched in her arms; she was holding the child when she met her death. Mother and child. We couldn't separate the two bodies, they were clutching each other so tightly.

"When we investigated the case we discovered that the owners—three hundred of them—had marched to the village in a group from the surrounding area. They were armed with guns, bird rifles and similar weapons. They attacked the men in the village, who took flight. When they saw the rifles and heard the shots, the men left their women and children and fled out into the fields. The poor women took shelter in the hut that belonged to the village leader.

"There had been disputes before between the farmworkers and the landowners. The poor had demanded higher wages. There had been fights before and one of the landowners had been killed. Now the landowners wanted revenge and wanted to scare the farmworkers.

"The hut where the women took shelter was an ordinary earth hut with a few bamboo poles that held up the roof. But that wasn't enough to burn up forty-four people. When we cremate our dead we need a lot of fuel. The landowners knew that; they brought flammable fluids with them, kerosene and such. They poured it on the hut.

"No one lives in the village anymore. The buildings are burnt out. It looks like a haunted place. Everything ended so tragically."

The Green Revolution

We had been in India several months when the murders in Kilavenmani occurred. We had also visited India before, three years earlier, and we believe we can now see changes that will have widespread consequences for India's future.

Today people talk about a "green revolution" in India—a result of the new agricultural policy. It is said that the problem of supplying food for more than five hundred million Indians will soon be solved and that rice may even be exported. The latest crops have yielded record harvests and people talk about an end to the famine years.

In discussions with the people responsible for the agricultural policy, we got a clear picture of the origin of the new policy. Gone was the socialistic rhetoric of the Nehru period. Gone was the talk about land reforms and thoroughgoing changes in distribution of rural power. Gone also was the talk about equality as an end and as a means for attaining the welfare of the many. We knew that this, to a large extent, had only been talk and very little action. A lot of talk but no action led, of course, to the great famine of 1966–67.

Agricultural technicians have replaced ideologues. The government wanted to help the peasants with new, more effective, breeds of rice and wheat, with fertilizers, irrigation and farming equipment. But those helped first are those considered to have the greatest ability to use help—their production figures are most important. As a result, resources are channeled first to the rich farmers—those with a great deal of land in the most developed regions of the most fertile states.

THE INDIAN VILLAGE—
INEQUALITY AS A SOCIAL SYSTEM

Eighty percent of India's population lives in the villages. A village consists, on the average, of less than one thousand people divided into a few hundred families.

The main feature of the village social system is the division of people into well-defined, hierarchically ordered groups. This system determines in detail how labor will be shared, how profits will be distributed, who has political power in the village, and what status each group has. The villager, once born into a group, can never leave it. Thus it is a person's birth that determines his welfare, power and standing in the village; what he has accomplished means little.

The various groups—the castes—are linked by an arrangement for the exchange of goods and services sometimes called the "jajmani system." This system decides, for example, that the members of a certain shoemaker-caste family are bound to perform their services for certain landowning families. They cannot refuse, and, if for any reason they cannot work, they must provide replacements. In return they receive a traditionally determined portion of the landowner's crop one or more times a year. In this way all the village craftsmen and farmworkers are tied to the village landowners in a traditional state of dependence—a situation which cannot be broken within the limits of the social system, a system which smacks of slavery.

The villagers mix only within their own caste and feel little solidarity with those outside the caste line. The social division is total.

But today not everyone submits to this system.

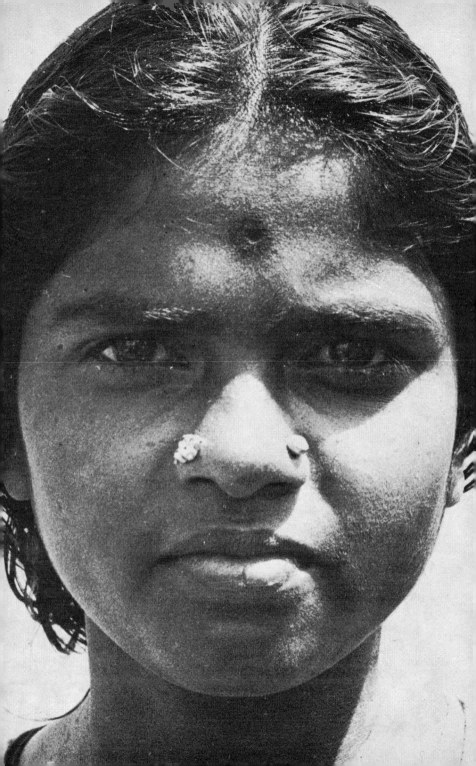

THE CASTE SYSTEM TODAY

The caste system still flourishes in India but its function has changed in many ways during recent years. It works in different ways in the country and in the city, and the caste system in the countryside changes in step with the changing economic system.

Traditionally those castes which had religious power in the villages also had political and economic power. They were landowners, though often not farmers. Now other castes are beginning to supplant them—the landowning and farming castes which are better able to employ the new farming methods and thereby increase their economic power and thus also their political power.

Rural politics is often conducted along caste lines. People feel loyalty toward their caste and vote as the leader of the caste—the caste adviser—decides. They vote preferably for politicians who belong to their own caste. The castes become voting blocs and politicians often appeal to caste interests.

But this and a proletarization of the villages on the heels of the new agricultural economics is leading to the beginning of awareness among the low castes that they are exploited. They are beginning to cross caste lines, conscious of their mutual situation.

Antagonisms between castes are changing into class antagonisms.

Growing Antagonism

We find growing antagonisms in Indian society. In several places around the country, the peasants have revolted and fighting has broken out. In the cities, riots and the persecution of minorities have become more common.

Close to four-fifths of India's population lives in the countryside and is more or less directly employed in agriculture. Shouldn't the increased production have lessened the unrest in the countryside? What does the "green revolution" mean for the peasants? What lies behind the clashes between the rich and poor farmers we see reported more and more often in the Indian newspapers?

In order to get an answer to these questions, we traveled to the Thanjavur district in southern India. Thanjavur was the model area for rice production in the country, and it is one of the areas where the new agricultural policies have been in operation longest and been most successful.

Kilavenmani is in Thanjavur.

In India it is primarily the state governments that deal with agricultural policy. Therefore, we asked Mr. Prabhakar, who is responsible for agriculture in the state of Tamil Nadu* where Thanjavur is located, to explain agricultural policy.

We puzzle our way through the ministry: stairs, corridors, a thousand doors to pass, a thousand chairs to sit and wait on before we go farther, a thousand servants who show the way and take one another's places—all these servants, short and dark with timid eyes, padding along noiselessly, quickly, in front of us, turning about occasionally to check that we're still following, occasionally waving a hand to the side, "this way."

Finally we arrive, wait on chairs outside a room into which

* Formerly called Madras.

24

we are then sent to sit on more chairs where we wait until we are led in to the minister. He is sitting at the other end of a huge room, behind an enormous desk; a gigantic mural on the wall behind him depicts some children in front of a rice field. He is wearing a yellow nylon shirt with a fountain pen in the breast pocket and has black eyeglasses—a small variant on the bureaucrat's uniform. He is very friendly, speaks quickly and clearly and manages to cover a lot of ground during the quarter of an hour before he goes off to a meeting with his thick briefcase under his arm.

—The first and second five-year plans succeeded very well in the agricultural area, the main reason being our luck with the weather. The third five-year plan, however, was a total failure.

We have now concentrated more of our resources on agricultural production. During the fourth five-year plan, starting in 1968–70, our most important goal will be to spread the new highly productive breeds of rice introduced in India a couple of years ago. We have, however, had certain difficulties in adapting them to our circumstances.

We have problems with irrigation. The only region in our state with a reliable water source is the rich delta in the Thanjavur district. There we can use these new miracle rices, so we have chosen the district as a model area for our new agricultural policy. We invest as much as we can in this area. Then there are work-force problems. In the future we will be using more and more mechanized labor. The number of tractors, for example, has increased quickly here.

—How is land distributed here?

—We have a law that provides that no one may hold more than thirty acres for agricultural use.

—Does the law work?

—In practice it is true that a lot of land has quite suddenly been signed over to relatives and friends, etc.

25

—But isn't your new agricultural program too heavily directed toward technical solutions and too little toward other essential institutional factors? It has been said that the only way to solve the problems of Indian agriculture is to break the power of the landowners, the moneylenders, and the merchants.

—Quite right. We have, through increased state credit assistance, tried to lessen dependence on the traditional moneylenders. Is that sufficient as an answer?

—Yes, in regard to credit. What about the black market and landowning?

—Yes, well, I have my own opinions. They aren't the government's opinions. The farmworkers must be prepared to stand on their own feet much more than they can now. The faster they learn it, the faster we'll be able to have the "green revolution," as we call it.

In Thanjavur

How do those who administer the new program see their roles and what do they think are the important parts of the program? One of the chief administrators, P. K. Aiyasamy, explained:

—We call this a package deal. It was devised by the Ford Foundation. It has two components: first, we are trying to extend the use of better seed, fertilizer, pesticides, agricultural machinery, and so on; second, we are offering a service package—we give the farmers scientific agricultural advice. We aim completely at increasing productivity. It has now increased from two thousand to twenty-two or twenty-three hundred pounds per acre.

We're trying to introduce a new high-productivity, quick-growing rice breed which requires more fertilizer. Then we can grow two crops per year on a great portion of the land. We also extend credit to the farmers. We're trying to expedite the distribution of irrigation so that the water can be used as much as possible.

—How much has this increased productivity cost?

—Cost? You mean how much has this project cost? That I don't know.

—Approximately how large a part of the population here owns land and how large a part are farmworkers without any land at all?

—That I can't answer. It varies. There is no concentration of land in a few hands since there is a law that forbids the possession of land past a certain limit. There are three hundred thousand landowning families and 1.2 million acres of cultivated land. That means only three to four acres of land per family, but I have no idea how many have no land at all.

—Have you had difficulty in your work trying to persuade farmers to follow your advice?

—In the beginning we had certain problems, but now it's easier. We have succeeded in covering the entire area with a new seed, and 60 to 70 percent with fertilizer. Now we have the farmers' trust.

—How does your credit-lending plan work?

—We give approximately two hundred fifty rupees per acre to the rice producers. Of this, one hundred sixty rupees are in the form of goods—for example, fertilizer or seed. The cultivator gets the rest in cash to cover crop-connected expenses. Then he pays this back after the harvest, or after one year with 7 percent interest.

—How many have received this credit?

—I'm not familiar with that figure.

—Has your giving of credit displaced traditional money-lenders?

—Yes, it has in a way.

—What have the moneylenders done about it?

—They have their own clientele. These moneylenders will always be around; they are a necessary evil that can never be gotten rid of. The moneylender is not just a moneylender—he is a kind of institution. He offers so many other services. He is a friend, a philosopher—he leads the farmer. He is like a friend, a relative. He is always at hand, there isn't a lot of unnecessary red tape.

(We tried in vain to find out which groups had gotten most out of the program, which had lost, how the farmworkers' wages had changed, if land distribution had changed, what lay behind the murders in Kilavenmani. But Aiyasamy only answered:)

—We are agricultural experts. We don't concern ouselves about who is a landowner or a farmworker. We are just trying to increase productivity.

Peasant Rebellions

In Thanjavur in recent years increasing numbers of farm-workers and peasants have begun to organize themselves to improve their situation. This is something new. It has never happened to this extent since India became independent in 1947. In several recent cases the organizing drive has taken the form of armed struggles between the landowners and the poor. The antagonisms are sometimes so violent that they are hard to imagine—one example is what happened in Kilaven-mani.

We spoke with one of the farm leaders in the area, M. Kathamuthu. He is a small man, dressed in a white *kurta* that shines as brightly as the generous smile on his black, dried-out face. He tells us that he is casteless, that he began as a peasant and is now a farm leader. Sometimes he is bitter, sometimes full of ardor.

We asked what were the most important problems of the poor.

—The farmworkers' wages. They have increased during recent years, but not as much as the cost of living, so in effect the wages have decreased. The landowners hold onto the crops until there is a shortage of food. Then they can get higher prices for them. But this is only possible for landowners with a lot of land, with surplus acreage.

In other words, the landowner creates a kind of serf, although it is forbidden. He does this by giving a worker a loan of fifty rupees. The farmworker can never pay it back. In this way he becomes bound to the landowner, who can use him when he wants, to perform odd jobs for only half or a third of the normal wage.

The land is very unequally distributed. Approximately one-fourth of the rural population has no land at all; 40 percent are tenants. Of the landowners, the majority have such small plots that they don't suffice to support their families. The land reforms haven't been effective, there are too many loopholes in the laws.

Then there is the housing problem for farmworkers. They live in their houses at the landowners' whim. They don't own their own homes or the land they stand on. The landowners can evict them whenever they wish.

—Are the poor helped by the package program?

—The package program helps primarily the upper class of the community; its main goal is to improve production, not to improve the social system. Loans are made, but who gets the loans? Only the large landowners. All this is increasing.

The landowners are now trying to get back as much land as possible. Farming has become profitable. After a dry year it is often difficult for the tenants to pay rent; the landowners use this as an excuse to take back the land. The number of families without land is increasing quickly, there are so many ways for the rich to confiscate the land. The landowners use their economic power to bring in farmworkers from other parts of the country when their own workers want higher wages. It has gotten restless here. Look at Kilavenmani, for example.

Here in Thanjavur, the temple also owns a lot of land. It is difficult to find any exact figures since even the government hesitates to examine temple landholdings. One organization here has seventy thousand acres, although some of it is outside of this district. The religious organizations usually rent their land to large landholders who in turn sublet to smaller tenants.

—What power do the moneylenders have?

—The government and the cooperatives give only 30 to 40 percent of what is needed. It is the common people who must cast their lot with the moneylenders. They usually ask two sacks of rice as interest on a hundred-rupee loan, which corresponds to fifty rupees in interest for one year. Sooner or later the poor come in debt to the moneylenders—maybe during a period of famine, or because of a marriage or something similar.

The rich here have improved their situation. Greater production brings in more money. They can lend out part of the profit at high rates of interest. They can afford to hold back a portion of the crop until prices rise. There are so many ways to earn money if one has money. The landowners also try to pay wages in cash instead of in goods since prices are rising.

—What do they use this money for?

—They don't invest it so much in land; they buy stocks. Some of the richest landowners invest in sugar refineries and convert their whole farm production from rice to cane sugar.

It has also become common to invest in movie theaters.

—Most farmworkers are casteless. Are there caste antagonisms between them and the high castes?

—The caste system is still strong here. The old taboo that a Brahman may not touch a casteless person—an Untouchable—is still followed strictly. The casteless are regarded as unclean. But in a way this is changing. When it comes to political struggles, the poor are now beginning to cross over caste lines.

Without doubt, a radicalization is now taking place. The poor have many common goals and difficulties regardless of caste or religion, and this has begun to bring them together toward a common platform.

Bastin, Farmworker

What about the farmworkers themselves? What do they think about their own situation and their future?

Bastin, a farmworker:

"I am about forty years old. There are nine people in the family my wife and I support. We live in the same house I was born in, ten miles from here. My wife and I earn the same amount, three and a half rupees a day. One month of the year we get our wages in the form of rice. I own two oxen, but no land. I would like to have two acres, it would be enough.

"The government must take the land and divide it up among the people. We will never get any land directly from the landowners. I am poorer today than I was ten years ago. We don't have enough food and clothing. It can't go on like this. We must get our own land. My village has thirty huts. Two hundred people live here, all casteless farmworkers, four or five of us own land. In another part of the village, a mile or two from us, live twenty families belonging to castes. They all have land."

He is standing in the field with the sun glaring on his face, which glistens with sweat. In his hand he holds a hoe with which he emphatically pounds the ground now and then while he talks, turned toward the interpreter. While the interpreter translates for us, Bastin looks at us carefully. He is bare-chested, dressed in a *dhoti*, a white cotton cloth wrapped like a skirt and drawn up between his legs so he can move more freely. Behind him stand about ten farmworkers, men and women, listening. They stand completely quiet, with tools in their hands, and nod occasionally while Bastin speaks. They are looking at us the whole while.

Swamajh, Farmworker

"We get different pay for different jobs. We can get work only during part of the year; the rest of the year, we're jobless. Sometimes we can get work cleaning the irrigation canals and such, then we get two rupees per day.

"I have a wife, three daughters and a son. The pay I get lasts during the period I have work. Sometimes I can save a little that will last a few extra days, but not more than a week. When I can't get work, the money doesn't last. If I don't get work, we starve, but in some way we've managed until now. I had a little land before, but I lost it. Besides food I need about one rupee a day for other expenses."

We're sitting in the middle of Alangudi, a village in the Thanjavur district. It is harvest time, but the village population has left the green fields for a while; they all want to look at us. They follow us laughing when we go through the village and look, they stand seriously around us when we ask them how it is to live here. The women stand separate from the men; the children take cover behind the women's gleaming saris. They live in simple earthen huts with palm branch roofs, exactly as people lived in Kilavenmani. We feel, everyone feels, that what happened there could easily happen here.

food and power:
the agricultural economy

In an underdeveloped country like India, the amount of agricultural production determines the standard of living for the majority of the people. Agricultural production *has* increased during the period of independence. But the average yearly increase in the harvest between 1950-51 and 1965-66 was only 1 percent greater than the annual population growth (2 percent) during the same fifteen-year period. Production per person, then, grew hardly at all.

Behind these facts is a painful implication for the future. That production could keep pace with the population growth at all simply resulted from the great increase of cultivated acreage. Such growth cannot continue forever. Agricultural production can be increased in two ways only: by extending the cultivated acreage, or by improving the productivity of already cultivated earth. As the first possibility diminishes, productivity must be greatly increased if production per person is not to be decreased.

It must be added that, for many reasons, Indian statistics are rather unreliable. Information given by official sources is often false or misleading. These sources wish to hide the country's real problems and so an exaggeratedly optimistic picture of its development is often painted. Official publications of the last twenty years are full of hopeful predictions about development—predictions which have most often been proved wrong. Unlike many other Asian nations, India does have both a developed system for the gathering of statistics and a great many well-educated statisticians. But because of the large differences in income between the various classes and between different parts of the country, the average figures for increases in agricultural production, for example, give a misleading picture of changes in the living standards of the poor. In addition, the principles, definitions and theories employed have been adopted from industrially developed nations, and are therefore sometimes quite useless in a country like India. The researchers are often Westerners or wealthy Indians educated in Europe or America. They have little or no contact with the problems of the poor majority, and their research is often colored by upper-class values. (Daniel and Alice Thorner's book *Land and Labour in India* [1962] is recommended to those who wish to study the effect of these factors upon Indian agricultural statistics.)

Technical Factors

Productivity in Indian agriculture is, generally speaking, low—among the lowest in the world. But this is not a function of the soil quality. Low productivity has technical causes, which, in turn, have institutional causes. In other words, low productivity is caused by the ownership situation, the marketing and credit systems, and so forth.

We shall begin with the technical causes. Charles Bettelheim, in his analysis of the Indian economy, *India Independent* (1968), gives four technical reasons why productivity was so low when the country gained independence: poor water access, lack of fertilizers, overabundance of live-stock, and poor farming techniques.

It is not true that it rains too little in India (the average is forty-eight inches per year). The problem is that the precipitation is so unevenly distributed, both in time and in location. What is needed, therefore, is not only artificial irrigation, but also reliable water control—a method of getting the right amount of water to the right fields at the right time. At most one-fourth of the cultivated soil will have reliable water control by the end of the fourth five-year plan in 1974. It is expected that the present productivity of these fields will have doubled by that time.

The arable land suffers a shortage of fertilizers as crucial as the lack of water. Many forests in the more populated areas have been felled, which has led to the use of cow dung as fuel instead of fertilizer. The organic wastes of humans and animals are used only rarely as fertilizer, and industrially produced fertilizer is too expensive for any but the richest farmers to buy.

Nothing is put forward so often as the root of nearly all evil in India as the "sacred cows." The fact is, quite simply, that there *are* too many cows (and oxen, bulls and buffalo) in India. They graze too much of the plant cover in proportion to what they produce in the form of milk, power, and dung. If there were fewer animals, they would give more milk and draw loads better. But this animal overpopulation does not depend entirely or even mainly upon the Hindu taboo against the slaughter of cows, as is commonly believed in the rest of the world. The problem is actually an economic one. All those cows, apparently roaming around on the loose, are in fact owned by individuals. If a poor family has anything at all of economic value in this world, it would most likely be one or two cows. These cows provide the family with the only fuel it can afford—fuel with which to cook its rice or warm the cottage at night. They also provide the family with a valuable protein source—milk. Even if this seems very little, it is necessary for the sustenance of life. Cows can be used as plow animals in farming. A pair of oxen is easily worth several years' wages for a poor peasant. It is therefore of no use to point out to him that the country would be better off in the long run if he killed one of his cows. It would be a catastrophe for him. In order to ensure that the welfare of the individual peasant and the country are not at odds, changes must be made in some essential lifestyles.

An estimated three-quarters of the population is unable to read and write and no one knows how many cannot add and subtract—an ability very important to the impoverished farmer in the jungle of merchants and lenders. This complicates the dissemination of modern agricultural methods. The English never intended that the Indian people should learn to read, write and count. The education the English gave the Indians was intended to provide administrators and people who could help the colonialists rule.

It is often said that Indian farmers are so tradition-bound that they are simply not interested in new methods that could increase crop yields (see Kusum Nair's *The Indian Villages*). The experience of the Thanjavur project demonstrates the opposite. There is certainly a skeptical attitude toward new methods, but this attitude has little to do with tradition or religion. A peasant with a plot of a few acres risks his life if his crop goes bad. In that situation, the farmer does not gamble. If some "expert" comes along who has never worked the land himself and suggests a change in a centuries-old process, it is not so strange for the farmer to demand some evidence. Skepticism all too often proves itself to be well grounded, since many of the improved methods have been devised in quite different circumstances (often in the United States or Russia) and would lower Indian crop yields.

An even more important obstacle to change lies in the institutionalized relationships that often make increased production less profitable for the grower or the landowner-merchant-moneylender.

The Colonial Heritage

The agricultural policies of the British colonialists in India brought deep and serious consequences in the early nineteenth century for the people of the countryside. The soil was made a commodity which could be privately owned. At least in theory, this had not previously been possible. Now the land could be bought and sold; the landowner was required to pay tax to the English. The landowner could in turn let the land for an even higher rent, thus acquiring an income without labor. The tenant himself might rent out the land and there are stories about scores of such middlemen between a landowner and a completely exploited farmer.

Another drastic change brought about by the British was the increased commercialization of farming, beginning in the middle of the nineteenth century. Agriculture was altered gradually from production for family or village consumption to production for sale. There were several reasons for this. The modified ownership conditions increased the economic demands of the state on the farmer, and the landowners forced the peasants to sell their crops for cash. Another reason was that British policy deliberately sought to bring the commercialization about. England after the Industrial Revolution needed raw material for its industries and markets for its goods. The English built Asia's most extensive railway network in India and thus linked the interior of the country with the port cities and, by steamship, with England.

All this opened undreamt-of opportunities for the money-lenders. Rather inconsequential previously, they kept pace with the expanding commercialization and the money needs of the countryside's key figures; their power grew accordingly. From the middle of the nineteenth century, land values rose, partly because increased population made the soil a more and more scarce commodity. The result was often that the lenders used their power to claim the land as well as to take the crops.

The rising rents, commercialization, centralization of land-holding, and oppression led to a series of widespread famines, which were worsened by the competition of British textiles with Indian weavers in the cities and perhaps, to a certain extent, with those in the countryside.

Because of this colonial and domestic exploitation, the farm surplus—that part of the production which the farmers themselves did not use—could never be used for industrialization. The surplus was exported or used by the upper classes for luxury consumption.

Nehru's Agricultural Policy

The Indian villages have thus been rocked by violent upheavals during the last few centuries—the same villages that so many outsiders have described as unchanging for thousands of years. In fact, they are only unchanging in the sense that the poor of the villages have scarcely had their lot improved since independence in 1947. On the contrary, the number of poor people has increased, and they have become even more impoverished than during the era of British rule. (The Thorners refer to a study that shows that per capita foodstuff production sank 32 percent during the fifty years immediately preceding independence.

From 1947, when Nehru became prime minister, until the early 1960s, official agriculture policy was directed at changing the institutionalized relationships in the countryside. The land reforms were to be an important remedy. They would—it was said—break the landlords' power and give the soil to those who worked it. Since the constitution gives the states the right to legislate agricultural law, the land reforms varied in form in the different states. But a constant theme was the limiting of landholdings. This limit varied from state to state—for example, in 1961 the limit was fifteen acres in Kerala and two hundred sixteen acres in Andhra Pradesh. In some states consideration was also given to the quality of the land.

But it is no longer even an official secret that the land reforms were a complete fiasco from the viewpoint of the poor. There were far too many loopholes in the laws passed by the state parliaments, which are, by and large, forums for the landholders. In the villages, no one could push through decisions that went against the landholders' interests. The land reforms, like cooperatives, were of no use to the poor majority. The reforms did change the landowning situation for various groups among the landowners: Land ownership has passed from a group of landlords who lived in the cities or abroad to those who live close to their land. This does not necessarily mean that the former group has lost its power, since it received economic compensation for lost land and thereby capital to exploit the poor further. Kotovsky writes about this group in *Agrarian Reforms in India* (1964): "They occupy a stronger position [than before] in the sphere of circulation—in the farm produce market and agricultural credit." He continues, ". . . the development of credit and other forms of agricultural cooperatives has strengthened the position of the capitalist elements in the countryside. Investigations of the activity of the cooperatives have shown that they are run by the landlords and the upper crust of the peasantry, who in the main use them in their own interests."

Institutional Factors

1. *The distribution of landholding* among the rural population is the factor which more than any other decides the situation in the countryside. But if the statistics are at any point misleading, it is at this sensitive spot. Questions are asked and answers given so that they serve the interests of the questioner or respondent. One example is taken from the most recently published National Sample Survey, 17th Round, for the year 1961–62. If the figures for acreage offered for rent and acreage rented are compared, the first reads fourteen million acres and the second thirty-five million. That the main reason for this enormous difference is the landowners' attempt to avoid the land reform legislation is rather obvious. Since one of the goals of this legislation has been to give the land to those who use it, there is every reason for the man who offers land to rent to hide this fact from the authorities. It is not even certain that the figure for rented land is correct, because the tenants are surely afraid to admit the true situation—it might lead to punishment by the landowners.

The Thorners describe India's agrarian relationships as the most complex in the world. For several reasons, it is nearly impossible to grasp the landowning distribution. There are many different kinds of ownership, which differ from section to section of this enormous country and from season to season. There are various levels of tenants, each of whom may own land himself while leasing acreage of a different quality. The landholder can be a small farmer with poorer holdings than an agricultural laborer, or an almost-feudal landlord, or a capitalist landowner who runs his farm according to the latest scientific discoveries, with strict corporate economics as a model.

(a) On the lowest rung of the social ladder in the Indian village stands the *agricultural laborer.* He is lowest both economically and socially. He owns no land, or too little land to be able to support a family. Wages vary between different parts of the country and between different seasons. An agricultural worker in Punjab can earn perhaps two dollars an hour while daily wages elsewhere are only ten cents. The average income per person in an agricultural worker's family is only about $14 *per year*, which is approximately 40 percent of the average personal income in the nation. The percentage of agricultural workers within the population has increased since independence, and they constitute probably 40 to 50 percent of the agrarian population—but they own perhaps 5 percent of the land.

The vast majority of agricultural workers are casteless or of low caste. They are bound by the tyranny of the caste system to work for certain landowning families for wages in cash or in the form of part of the crop. This is in some areas a form of outright slavery, sometimes called *begar*; it has, however, been replaced more and more by regular wage-labor. The agricultural workers are despised, economically exploited, and without political influence.

(b) Above them in the village hierarchy comes the various *tenant groups*. Tenants rent land either by oral or by written contract, most often from a landlord who lives nearby. They pay rent either with a fixed share of the crop—often around 50 percent—or with cash. As indicated above, they are probably underrepresented in the statistics, but there is no doubt that their share of the farming population has decreased. This

is due partly to the land reforms, which forced many landowners to tend the crops themselves in order to keep their
land, and partly to the increased profitability of farming in
some areas, which has encouraged owners to farm themselves
rather than rent out the land. The tenants now constitute
perhaps 20 percent of the agrarian population. They are
fairly evenly divided between the casteless, low castes, and
middle castes, and are also slightly represented among the
high castes.

(c) The middle peasants—*peasant proprietors* who tend
their plots without hired workers—constitute the next category. Their holdings usually fall somewhere between four and
fifteen acres. These *kisan*s are forced to sell part of their
produce for regular expenses and to make certain purchases.
Like the first two groups, they must sometimes borrow
money. They make up one-third or a little more of the agricultural sector and own land in about the same proportion.

(d) The last group is the *landlords*. These hold more than
fifteen acres and must use agricultural workers or rent out
land. Their portion of the agricultural population is about 10
percent, but they own more than half of the cultivated
acreage. Some of them, so far only a small minority, pursue
capitalist farming: the work is carried out by hired laborers
with modern farming methods and modern implements,
maximum profits being the goal. The majority are landlords
of a more feudal type.

2. In close connection with the landlords work the *moneylenders,* more than half of whom are themselves landowners.
The moneylenders are also tied to the general financial
interests in the cities. State and cooperative credit lending has
of course increased since independence, but it reaches
primarily the rich peasants. A large number of the small plots
run at a loss because they are too small—half of the farms
encompass only 6 percent of the cultivated acreage and are

unremunerative. Thus the small farmer quickly becomes indebted to the village moneylender—the only person to whom he can turn when he needs money. It is estimated that between one-third and one-half of the farmers are indebted to village moneylenders. It is a common misconception that the loans are for "unnecessary" expenses such as marriage. In reality, the most common reason for the loan is that the borrower is starving and needs money for food. A study in Bengal in 1946–47 showed that more than 70 percent of loans to agricultural workers were for food. (This was also the most common reason for borrowing by tenants and middle peasants.) Only 6 percent of the agricultural workers' loans were for social or religious reasons; loans to middle peasants for such purposes were 10 percent of the total. (The study is published in Bhowani Sen's *Evolution of Agrarian Relations in India*.)

Since 85 percent of the farmers' loans come from private moneylenders, these men hold a position of tremendous power in the countryside. Interest rates on the loans are very high—often around 50 percent, and even higher rates are not uncommon. It is therefore very difficult for a poor farmer who goes into debt ever to be free of it. Often he must pay interest for the rest of his life, and he becomes completely dependent on the moneylender, who is often the landlord as well.

The lender works with the financial interests in the cities and gets some of his resources from them. Bettelheim writes about this cooperation: "The connection creates a long chain of interests which unite big monopoly and financial capital with rural moneylending capital. Their solidarity is one of the reasons why the different measures designed to reduce the peasantry's dependence on moneylending capital have had little effect until very recently. The most moderate of such reforms—notably the extension of cooperative agricultural credit based on the credit of the State Bank of India—have met with little success."

3. The third member of the powerful triumvirate of the villages is the *merchant.* Since there is usually only one merchant in the area, he has a monopoly over local business and can in general manipulate prices. The merchant's activities cause the price of foodstuffs in the villages to fluctuate seasonally. At harvest time the merchant offers low prices for the crops of the smaller farmers, who are forced to sell a large part of their harvest in order to meet certain steady expenses and to buy those necessities they cannot produce themselves. Later in the year, the merchants (and richer peasants who can afford to hold onto their crops) sell back the food at considerably higher prices. These seasonal variations invite speculative capital from the city to the countryside; the profits can reach 50 percent within a few months.

With increased agricultural commercialization, the merchants' power has increased correspondingly. Holding back goods over a large area in an organized fashion, they can create artificial shortages to push prices up still further. The great famine in Bengal in the early forties was caused partly by such activities.

The Roots of Underdevelopment

The position of this ruling triumvirate is the reason for the underdevelopment of Indian agriculture. It is because of the restrictive and oppressive influence of the landlords, moneylenders and merchants that agricultural production is so low and that so little of it serves those who need it. This influence, in turn, is the reason that India's enormous natural resources have not been put to use and that industrialization has not lightened the population pressure on the countryside, saving hundreds of millions from hunger and starvation.

The quasi-feudal relationships in the countryside therefore affect agricultural production mainly in two ways: (1) Production is restricted so that the natural opportunities are not fully exploited—productivity is low. (2) The surplus—that part of the produce which those who till the soil do not use themselves—which is produced despite these obstacles is taken by the landlords, moneylenders, and merchants, and is not used for investments in future production.

1. The amount of production is affected in many ways by extensive exploitation. The landlords can push the wages of agricultural workers to the absolute subsistence minimum, because their power in the village has seldom been restricted by organized resistance from the poor. Thus the laborers are undernourished and malnourished and cannot complete a full day's work. Tenants may pay such high rents that the balance of their earnings is not sufficient to feed their families. Even small farmers and middle peasants have difficulty working because of inadequate nutrition. Exploited by the merchants and moneylenders, they too cannot fill their stomachs.

The high rents and the custom of paying rent with a fixed percentage of the crop make it unremunerative to improve the soil. The tenant must pay for all artificial fertilizers himself, but he gets back only part of the increased production.

If the state or foreign aid starts a development program, it is primarily the rich landlords who enjoy the benefits and prevent the poor farmers from partaking of them. This means that village rulers do not permit harvests to increase to a point where prices decline and the poor become economically independent. Let us refer to an example investigated by the Thorners—the effects of an irrigation system in northern India, "The Weak and the Strong on the Sarda Canal":

"The canal water comes down to the villages through a

system of branches, distributaries, and minors. In the distributaries and minors there are placed pipes of various diameters (4", 5", 6", etc.) . . . 8' or 10' long. Through them the water spills into the small channels or water courses known as *guls* leading to the cultivated fields. Along both sides of the *guls* extend the fields of the 'weak' and the 'strong.' The maintenance of the *guls* depends, in practice, upon the mass of the ordinary cultivators, the 'weak.' Since they get inferior water service, they have little incentive to maintain the *guls* properly. When they do not maintain the *guls* properly, no one else does either. The *guls* become grassy, shallow (there is a major silting problem on Sarda), meandering, broken. Such *guls* waste a great deal of water. . . . Throughout the Sarda system it is the general rule—there are of course some exceptions—that the strong, the powerful, the well-connected . . . dominate the use of irrigation water. They get water first and they tend to take as much of it as they please. Only after they are satisfied do they permit the mass of ordinary, unimportant, petty cultivators to have access to it. . . . The ordinary peasants do not seem to have received the cumulative benefits of regular irrigation."

The landlord, merchant, and moneylender have no interest in seeing production increase, since this does not mean that their profits will increase thereby. The landlord does not want any competition when he sells his goods. The merchant wants the small farmers and agricultural workers to be in such need of goods that he can determine prices himself. The lender doesn't want the peasants to be independent—he doesn't really want them to repay their loans, since it is the lifelong interest payments from which he profits most. It is this fact which is so important: *All of the village rulers profit more when the production of the small farmers is held down and the poor starve than when the countryside prospers.*

Since all surplus from the small and middle peasants' production is exploited by the village rich, these peasants have nothing to invest in fertilizers, seed, etc. If they wish to improve their farming, they must borrow money from the village lender at such high interest rates that the enterprise is scarcely practical for them. But, as Bettelheim has pointed out, this is not the only problem: "The moneylender, who is often the local merchant, is not likely to agree to loans which might lower sale prices by increasing the harvest. The higher the prices, the greater a merchant's profit. Even when there is no lending involved, the grain merchants often exert pressure on the peasants whose produce they buy to limit their output. It is difficult for the peasants to escape this pressure."

2. Well, someone may say, perhaps it's true that the landlords exploit the poor and prevent increases of production, but don't the rich invest their surplus and thereby cause development and higher income for the whole community?

The tragic answer is that the rich do not invest to any great extent. In the first place, only a tiny minority of landlords run their farms efficiently and according to modern profit ideas, and are what one might call capitalist farmers. These are concentrated mainly in Punjab, but there are also some in other states like Andhra Pradesh and Tamil Nadu. However, most landlords and rich farmers run their farms with outdated and unproductive methods since, *under the existing system, it is more profitable to them.*

Secondly, the rulers of the village do not invest their large surpluses in any productive sector. Capital is in general not invested in more effective farming or in small industries; money is invested instead in more profitable things like speculation in produce, moneylending (mainly for unproductive ends), movie theaters, etc., but especially in land. (This does not necessarily imply that this land will be used more efficiently.) Net (productive) investments in agriculture constitute no more than about 3 percent of net income from agriculture. This is of course the most important reason Indian agriculture is so unproductive and India is starving. It is not even true that large landholders invest more per acre than small landowners. It is rather the reverse (according to the few studies which have been made) that is true. Investments are inversely proportional to the size of property holdings—the small farmers invest more than the large.

Paradoxes in Indian Agriculture

It is these *institutionalized* relations that have led to what the Indian economist Boudhayan Chattopadhyay has called "the paradox that is India." This paradox, consisting of many different paradoxes, has made it difficult for Western "experts" to make Indian reality agree with their theories about the ways in which society functions—in this case, of how an agrarian economy functions. Among the more important paradoxes in the Indian economy, according to Chattopadhyay's reasoning, are the following:

1. Despite the most sweeping land reform legislation in two centuries, the distribution of land is as concentrated as ever.

2. The areas of India where land owning is most concentrated show no higher productivity than those where holdings are less concentrated.

3. Large farms do not bring greater productivity.

4. Large farms do not enjoy appreciably greater stores of capital than small farms.

5. Areas with large landholding concentrations do not have a greater proportion of hired agricultural workers than areas with less farming.

6. Large farms have divided the land into small plots to as great an extent as small farms have.

7. Increased commercialization in the agrarian economy has not brought more efficient farming; rather it has increased the various kinds of precapitalist exploitative forms.

8. These effects of increased commercialization have been strengthened by the direction of the Indian educational system and the motivations it creates.

9. The ties between the large farms and moneylending increase with the growth of outstanding loan debts.

10. A general commercial explosion has not been followed by any general production explosion. This is due to the investing habits of the great landlords—the 10 percent of the farmers who control approximately 75 percent of the marketed produce.

The Consequences of the New Agricultural Policies

It is against this background that the new agricultural policies and the "green revolution" must be seen.

To do as the Indian government is now doing—substituting technical aid to certain large farmers in the wealthiest regions for thoroughgoing institutional changes—will never solve the problems of the poor.

This investment in at most 10 percent of the country's cultivated area will certainly increase harvest on these farms. The crop increase will be mainly in wheat and, to a considerably lesser extent, in rice (the new rice breeds have not enjoyed great success). Food for the poor and protein sources such as millet and chickpea have been completely neglected. The production increase of "poor man's food" has been only about 1.5 to 1.7 percent per year (well under the population growth rate), compared to an increase of 3.7 percent for wheat and 3.5 percent for rice.

A few well-to-do farmers will be able to produce a little

more wheat—"luxury food"—and thereby profit more. But this effect will not be felt in the rest of the economy. The poor will not have their lot improved; it is possible, however, that large famines can be avoided during the next ten years. Farm production will still be only a small fraction of what it could have been, and the surplus that can be scraped together by the starving workers and peasants will not be used to exploit the land resources.

World Bank economist Wolf Ladejinsky is one of the chief non-Indian experts on Indian agriculture. Let us fill out our experiences of the "green revolution" in Thanjavur with his summary of a study of a similar experiment in northern India—the Kosi area in Bihar:

"Till the other day, Purnea and Saharsa were very backward rural districts. With the Kosi irrigation scheme gradually coming into its own, they are less so now. Basic technological changes are taking place on holdings with assured water supply and for farmers with resources to acquire inputs other than water.

"The extension of wheat acreage and the rise in yields have been dramatic. The high-yielding paddy varieties have not done nearly as well but improvements may be anticipated.

"The green revolution is, however, limited as to both acreage and participants and this is likely to remain so even when the irrigation scheme is completed and the number of tubewells is vastly increased."

He describes how the conditions of tenants, agricultural workers and small farmers worsened or at best remained unaffected. He continues:

"It is not, however, the new technology which is the primary cause of the accentuated imbalances in the countryside. It is not the fault of the new technology that the credit service does not serve those for whom it was originally intended; ... that security of tenure is a luxury of the few;

that rents are exorbitant; that ceilings on agricultural land are notional; that for the greater part tenurial legislation is deliberately miscarried; or that wage scales are hardly sufficient to keep soul and body together.

"These are man-made institutional inequities."

food as weapon: the U.S.A.'s food assistance program

In a speech given March 23, 1961, American Secretary of Agriculture Orville Freeman said that food "has become a diplomatic weapon. Food is a means of persuasion. Food is power."

The shipment of food from the United States to India is a program of long standing. In 1949, when the Indian food situation had worsened, help was sought from the United States. Negotiations were prolonged and did not end until 1951. The main stumbling block was the U.S.'s condition that India alter its pro-Chinese policies. Only when strong public opinion built up within the States did the U.S. government give up its demands. The conditions of the agreement were very difficult for India: for this "aid"—wheat shipments—the country had to pay $105 per ton (the price on the U.S. domestic market was $93 per ton). The price was to be paid in hard cash (dollars); later it was decided that India would deliver its output of "strategic goods" in payment. At least half of the shipments had to be sent on American boats.

THE RULING TRIUMVIRATE IN THE COUNTRYSIDE

Land distribution in Indian agriculture is very lopsided. A few people own the greater part of the land—the best land. The majority of the rural population owns no land at all, or so little that they depend on working for the big landowners to eat.

The poor peasants and farmworkers, whose expenses during part of the year are often greater than their incomes, soon come into debt to the local moneylenders. Interest rates are very high—they run around 50 to 100 percent. The borrower's debt grows and with it his dependence on the moneylender. It is mainly the rich peasants who have benefited from state and cooperative credit lending.

The situation of the poor is made still worse by the local merchants' monopolistic control of food prices. At harvest time the poor cannot afford to wait until prices rise, but must sell their crop immediately at greatly reduced prices. Then at the end of the season, when the poor must buy food, the merchants raise their prices and get perhaps double what they paid a few months earlier.

The landowner, profiteer, and black marketeer have the power in the village. Often they are the same man, or if not they work together, which further worsens the position of the poor.

The most important stumbling block to making Indian agriculture efficient is the fact that the village rulers make more in their role of triple exploiter than by running an efficient farm.

THE GREEN REVOLUTION

In the face of stagnating agricultural production in the middle 1960s, the government modified its policy. Earlier, its goal was to help the poor by means of land reforms, cooperation, etc. But these "development" projects merely solidified the inequality of wealth and power. Now the government is trying to increase production through technological change, without harming the power structure.

Certain large farmers are helped with fertilizers, irrigation, better seed, increased lending, etc. Only the already wealthy in the most developed regions of the most fertile states are helped. This will perhaps enhance agricultural production; it will certainly increase inequality. The rich will get richer and the poor poorer. The differences of income between various parts of the country, already large, will grow larger; the regional tensions will increase.

Antagonisms in Indian society will grow.

In Kilavenmani, the casteless farmworkers tried to organize themselves, demanding their portion of the increased production. In revenge, the wealthy landowners in the area marched to the village, scared away the men, drove the women and children into a hut, poured kerosene on it and burned forty-four people to death.

This led private shippers to raise their charges from $10 to $25 per ton. Since nearly all the wheat was shipped on American-owned freighters, the United States earned $29 million in freight charges on the agreement.

Because of substantial subsidies to American agriculture, the United States after World War II had an oversupply of food that became acute at the beginning of the fifties. Domestic prices were high, and there would be no export opportunities unless prices were lowered to world market standards. The surplus grew and created great problems within the country. In order to solve these problems, President Eisenhower decided to sell the surplus at the going rate, and to accept payment in local currencies, since those countries which would consider buying couldn't pay in hard cash. A program was passed in 1954 under the title Public Law 480. The program's most important goal was thus to solve a difficult domestic problem; it succeeded in that task. American Secretary of the Treasury Douglas Dillon said in 1961 about the PL 480 programs, "They have helped us to get rid of surplus which would otherwise be difficult to maintain."

The first PL 480 agreement with India was signed in 1956, and during the following years it was renewed regularly. The first large-scale agreement was entered into on May 4, 1960, and covered the Indian purchase of sixteen million tons of wheat and one million tons of rice during a four-year period. The sale was to be at market prices, which were then rising—1961: 377 Indian rupees per ton, 1962: 394 rupees per ton, 1963: 463 rupees per ton, 1964: 425 rupees per ton.

According to this agreement, at least 50 percent of the freight was to be shipped on U.S. vessels; the United States made over $150 million during 1961–64, to be paid in hard cash. When surpluses of other commodities such as tobacco and cotton occurred, these were also included in the sales without consideration of India's need for them. In 1965, the control of PL 480 sales was transferred from the Department of Agriculture to the Department of State in order, according to President Johnson, to "further strengthen the Food for Peace program as an essential part of our foreign policy."

During the 1960s, the United States shipped large amounts of wheat to an India with severe food problems, an India where the rare good harvests seldom ended up feeding the starving. Quite naturally the U.S.'s grain deliveries to India have been represented as an extraordinarily kindhearted form of foreign aid.

India has had to pay for this "aid" with Indian rupees at continually inflating prices. This has led to the build-up of a tremendous American rupee reserve in India; in 1968 it contained twenty-two billion rupees—as much as the Indian government had in its possession. This money thus represents a great power factor in India, and with it the United States can direct a large part of Indian economic development. It is therefore of great interest to learn how the money has been used. According to the U.S. Information Service in New Delhi, of the money spent before July 22, 1968, approximately 20 percent went as gifts to the Indian government for various development projects, of which scarcely one-seventh went to develop industry and agriculture. Approximately 60 percent of the funds were lent to the Indian government. Loans to the official sector of industry have been avoided and less than a fourth of the loans went to agriculture.

Of the remainder, 7 percent were used to support American corporations in India and their daughter companies. Thirteen percent of the funds went to defray American "administrative" expenses—which probably means this aid to starving India finances the extensive American espionage network there. (There are many large and expensive research projects in India of the same type as the "Camelot" project in Latin America.* An extensive "sociological research study" along the northern border with China was revealed in 1968 in the Indian parliament.) The strategy for American usage of these huge funds is clear: its main object is to inhibit the development of a viable public sector in industry, instead reinforcing private capitalist efforts (primarily the large Indo-American corporations). Nor is there special interest in bolstering Indian agriculture in order to make the country self-supporting, something that would seem natural considering the money's source. Large amounts of the money have been used instead for an American cultural offensive on all levels, in the form of American teachers and schoolbooks, with a special emphasis on higher learning. With scholarships, exchange students, U.S.-supported research and instruction, etc., an attempt is being made to get a grip on the opinion-building process in the country.

India, unlike the Marshall Plan signers, has no co-decision right in the use of these twenty-two billion rupees. According to a November 1968 (and 1971) agreement, more than 40 percent of the sales money must be used to support Indian-American firms. In addition, India must make 80 percent of the payments in U.S. dollars.

The grain deliveries have also had an inhibiting effect on Indian agriculture by weakening the motivation of the Indian government to carry out thoroughgoing reforms—changing the ownership rights situation, forms of production, etc. In the big cities, where most of the wheat has been distributed, the opportunities for individual farmers to produce for sale have been reduced.

---

*A U.S. Defense Department–financed study, discontinued in 1966 after claims were made that the research was being used for counter-insurgency.

When India bought PL 480 wheat, the sales were accompanied by heavy political pressures. During the early fifties there was pressure on the country to change its pro-Chinese policy. Later, India was forced to give in to demands to break its trade agreements with North Korea and North Vietnam. In 1966, the United States succeeded in forcing India into a questionable devaluation of the rupee by threatening to cut off deliveries at a time when harvest catastrophes were plaguing the country.

THE CITIES
AND FASCISM

the cities

India is a country of shattered illusions, a country where the present has nothing to offer, where the future seems without hope, and where dreams of a glorious past are fantasy. Economic stagnation; tensions between various groups, areas, religions, castes, tribes and classes; memories of military defeats and subjection to foreign injustices—all these create overwhelming feelings of insecurity among much of the population.

During recent years this insecurity has fostered the growth of a number of different fascistic groups, most of them based on religious affiliation. The result of their activity has been a great increase in the number of riots and bloody battles in Indian cities—confrontations which, like the groups behind them, are different in different parts of the country. In north India, for example, most of the rioting is between Hindus and Muslims, though the riots seldom stem from religious disputes. Instead, they are often based on economic inequities; they are communalistic disputes—that is, conflicts between religious groups but with economic causes.

In today's India there is a gap between people's dreams and the reality in which they live, a gap that seems to be continually widening, and that is widest in the cities.

Since independence in 1947, economic development has indisputably taken place in India, but the fruits of development have not been divided equally. Those favored most are those already rich—landowners, industrial owners and top administrators. In the cities, those who have done less well include the large group of people usually called the middle class—office workers, civil servants, small businessmen and street vendors, craftsmen, schoolteachers, etc. Approximately half of India's city dwellers belong to this middle class— about fifty million people.

The overwhelming majority of the middle class are underpaid; they seldom earn more than forty dollars a month. They lack job security: often they can be fired arbitrarily— which may mean a long period without a job, living on what relatives can provide. Education is not, as it used to be, a guarantee of work; unemployed academics can now be counted in the millions rather than the hundreds of thousands. In Calcutta alone there are two hundred thousand unemployed academics. An antiquated educational system, created to fill the British colonial regime's need for low-ranking administrators, lures millions of students into working toward worthless degrees. Contacts with influential people are often more important than qualifications.

For the majority of the middle class, the quarter century since independence has not brought any economic improvement, considering the increased cost of living; on the contrary, their standing in relation to other groups has worsened.

A growing stream of people is drawn to the cities from the countryside. It is not primarily the poorest but usually the sons of the high caste and landowners who move to the city, either to get a status-giving education or because they are attracted by the opportunities to become consumers in the cities. A dedicated advertising industry constantly cultivates in these exploited people a need for luxury that only a small percentage of them can hope to satisfy. Here India's film industry probably plays an exceptionally important role. Small rural movie theater chains, where poor farmers and farmworkers can see a film for one or two cents, have turned out to be one of the most profitable areas of investment for the newly rich large landholders. The result is that the gospel of the Indian film industry, in living color and set to popular music, is spread throughout the countryside to defenseless peasants who have never been more than a few dozen miles from home. This is a film industry so thoroughly commercialized and reactionary that Satyajit Ray's seemingly harmless films—*Pather Panchali, The World of Apu*—can work as revolutionary detonators; it is a film industry which *never* depicts everyday Indian life or the problems of ordinary people but offers instead a falsified picture of the sweetness of wealth and dreams of getting rich quick.

Indian cities differ from their European counterparts during the early stages of industrialization in that they are consumption-oriented rather than production-oriented. The exodus from the countryside aggravates this problem—an unproductive middle class collects in the cities, and slum areas grow much more quickly than industries.

the civil servants
demonstrate in Delhi

The civil servants are demonstrating in Delhi for better working conditions, higher wages, job security, etc.—no uncommon demonstration. The unions are organizing: they will gather outside Indira Gandhi's palace in the evening to hear various political party representatives speak about the current civil servant situation.

It starts early in the afternoon. The city is big; long caravans stream in from all directions, a swarm of white shirts, the obvious uniform of the Indian civil servant—not the Indian *kurta,* but the European shirt, with a small fountain pen in the breast pocket. Add a small mustache and eyeglasses. Many have bicycles, the middle-class means of conveyance throughout India. No placards, a few banners, most with English text. Loud megaphones, clenched fists in the air. Police in khaki shorts and high turbans turn away traffic; the streets are not closed off except near the prime minister's residence where the various groups are meeting, crowding together, half a million civil servants in white shirts, a blend of decisiveness and fear in their eyes. All are men; not a single woman can be seen. The police patrol the crowd as well as they can, swinging their *lathi*s (the Indian equivalent of batons, made of bamboo).

Will the civil servants achieve anything with this demonstration? A half million pairs of eyes are directed toward the speaker. Far away over this white sea, over all the black, glossy haircuts, someone is standing and speaking to his party comrades, to his political opponents, to journalists, and perhaps to the five hundred thousand breadwinners listening to the loudspeakers.

private armies

There is a new unrest in India's cities today. It takes different forms in various parts of the country and in different situations. A demonstration of Delhi's civil servants can attract a half million or a million participants. Industrial workers' organizations are closing ranks behind a common program despite their ties to different parties. In West Bengal, the workers and large sections of the middle class have come together to bring the leftist communists into power in the state government. Even the very poorest—garbage collectors, rickshaw drivers, day laborers, for example—have in some places begun to organize on a class basis.

More common, perhaps, is communalism—association on the basis of religion, language, or region. All over India today people are organizing along communalist lines—and thus being channeled into the persecution of minorities by various fascistic groups.

There are now a number of such groups in India, many of them with a semi-military form of organization. Most of them have developed during the last two or three years and reflect the feelings of desperation and economic insecurity that are common among large groups in the country. It is primarily the poor middle class in the cities (but also parts of the working class) that are attracted by the fanaticism and simplistic solutions of these groups. The riots that have resulted have been particularly severe in the industrial areas; in the riots in Ranchi in the fall of 1967, for example, two hundred people were killed in anti-Muslim clashes. In the fall of 1969 more than five hundred people were killed in Ahmedabad. For many industrial workers, automation poses a real threat, making their everyday lives very uncertain; their desperation is easily steered into communalist antagonisms.

India's private armies are often quite openly supported by big industries which encourage their efforts to replace horizontal class solidarity with vertical group solidarities. Two of the largest private armies are RSS (Rashtriya Swayamsewak Sangh) and Shiv Sena. It is no secret that Birla* supports RSS and that Shiv Sena is supported by big business in Bombay. Instead of trying to change an unproductive and unjust economic system, these groups attempt to portray some minority as a dangerous enemy and thereby to turn desperation into hate and group antagonism. Instead of trying to build a better and more just future, they talk about a glorious past. The situation is complicated, however, because the group antagonisms are sometimes clearly class based. When DMK† in Tamil Nadu propagandizes for the Tamil language and talks about Indian imperialism, its accusation is based, both historically and economically, on hundreds of years of oppression.

* The Birla family owns the second largest Indian corporation—a Bombay-based industrial conglomerate. The Tata family owns the largest corporation.

† Dravida Munnetra Kazahagam, a mildly nationalistic socialist party in power in Tamil Nadu since 1967.

the sun shines high
and burning hot
over Madras

The sun shines high and burning hot over Madras. The air is heavy and close both outside and inside the railway station. A sickeningly sweet odor covers everything. Bearers—coolies in red shorts, blue shirts, and red turbans—stand waiting in silent groups, quiet as fragile plaster figures, or pad forward at a half-run with enormous loads on their heads, but with hopefulness on their sweaty faces. They are all small and black and thin.

Taxis with sleeping taxi drivers in khaki, rickshaws with sleeping rickshaw drivers—they all wait their chance outside the railway station. The rickshaw drivers: in some inexplicable way they manage to sleep, stretched out on the leaning carriages decorated with fringe and the OM symbol. Taxicabs with rich Indians inside drive up to the entrance now and then. The wealthy Indians are most often light of skin; with few exceptions they wear European dress—black trousers, pointed black shoes, white shirt with a shiny fountain pen in the breast pocket, mustache, eyeglasses, hair pomade, and a briefcase with many papers inside. Rickshaws with middle-class Indians come wheeling by now and then. The middle-class Indians are usually light-brown-skinned; usually they wear the same dress and accessories as the upper class, but slightly less expensive and simpler. They all look like copies of English bureaucrats; they prefer English to Tamil, at a restaurant they order "chips" rather than rice.

On the station floor lie the poor, poorer, poorest. In silent resting heaps they lie—men, women, and children, crowded together, directly on the floor or on a newspaper or a dirty towel. Here they lie and wait. How many are waiting for a train we don't know, but most of them aren't. They seem to be deep in sleep. When the trains squeal, loud and screeching, no one budges. Whatever they're waiting for, they've been waiting a long time.

"I shall teach myself and I shall raise myself up . . ."

"I shall teach myself and I shall raise myself up, that's always been my motto.

"When I started as a common worker, I got twenty rupees a month. That was forty-two years ago. I was seventeen years old then. After a few months I was head of the company. I taught myself more and made my way up. I've come a long way. I washed the office floor myself. I've never had any education, never went to college or the university. I've had to teach myself by long experience. Nothing can replace experience. Nothing can be taught with books that can't be taught better by experience.

"Now I own a company with six thousand employees. No one makes trouble. In ten years there haven't been any strikes to speak of. I treat my employees well.

"When the workers struck one time, they asked me if I wanted to talk things over with them, but I said no. If you want to strike, then strike, I said. If you come back to work we can talk about things. I won't discuss under threat. After three days they came back. I don't want to say that I gave the workers a lesson—no one can ever give the workers a lesson. They never learn.

"A worker in India can't help to make decisions for a company. No workers capable of it have evolved in India. How can a decision-making role be given to someone who only wants more and more, who demands more but who doesn't understand anything? You can't make a blind man see until you operate on him.

"It's like the third-class compartment on an Indian train: he who comes in prevents another from coming in. I must produce for my unemployed neighbors. Imagine that I earn one million rupees a year. Money has to be changed into something. You can't fill your stomach with money. As long as I exploit and invest in new factories and in this way give work opportunities to many people, what does it matter that I exploit? Let the cow grow and become fatted. Who doesn't exploit somebody? The United States, England, Sweden have grown up through exploitation; all countries have grown up through exploitation. Even Russia.

"Since July last year, I've been in a dilemma. I don't know if I will kill the workers or the workers will kill me. I'd like to shoot them all. They've nearly killed me already with all their demands. They've killed me. I'm losing money. I'd like to have a machine gun and shoot them all, but I don't know what to do, I need them. I hate them. It's their leader's fault, all of it. You can meet him one evening if you wish, he comes here every evening and wants to talk with me. They've killed me. They are stronger than I am. I'd like to kill them.

"I've always been interested in politics. I'm called a social-ist. I work actively as a socialist. Indian politics are dirty. They'll only be cleaned up when money doesn't matter. Nowadays, economics can't be separated from politics. A socioeconomic revolution in India couldn't hurt. But a simple political revolution would be bad both for the workers and for me—the government would have to be authoritarian and the workers would have to work like dogs for the government until they raised living standards.

"I think the government is acting wrong, they're mishandl-ing the money they have to develop the country. What's the use of building roads when there aren't any cars? What's the use of building expensive traffic bridges at railroad crossings so people don't get to the movie theater twenty minutes late, when people don't have enough food? Or of education, when most people don't have food, which is the most important, the essential, need of man? A hospital could be built for the money. All the planning is wrong; I've always accused my friends in the Congress of that. First we should see that people have food, then clothes, then health care, and then housing. I wouldn't place education higher than fifth.

"Law and order problems have increased recently. The communists have been more active during the last three years than ever. They have to start trouble. Take the student prob-lems, for example. How many students want trouble? The majority want peace and quiet, but there are maybe twenty troublemakers who start everything. They are communists and they make the other students join them, otherwise they threaten to knock them down.

"There is hardly any communalism in India. It is a delu-sion, an idea the government spreads. RSS is not, as many believe, a militant organization. It is not even anti-Muslim. I have many good friends who belong to RSS. I like to call them deeply devoted. It is not true RSS killed Gandhi. The government invented that. If they came to power in this country the politics would at least be clean and anticommunist. Perhaps they'll win more votes in the next election.

"The communists cause too much trouble in India. By the way, where is there communism? I've traveled in China, I know China, I was there in 1936. There, father eats son. They are cannibals. The Chinese and the Japanese, the whole race should have been atom-bombed a long time ago, they are the biggest danger on the earth today, they should have been exterminated. I've heard stories about how the Chinese in Shanghai speared small children on long poles and held them up in the air and showed them to people. The whole race is a danger to humanity. They should have been killed a long time ago to save people today. I don't know. Now it is too late, perhaps. They're stronger than we are. That is why they must be gotten rid of. No, I am not a fascist; I am a sensitive person. Sensible. No one can be more sensitively nationalistic than I. Patriotic. You don't understand this. You belong to another race—I don't say your race is worse, I only say it is different. Chinese people are all born a special way. Likewise Indians. Likewise Swedes. And Negroes. I have been in the United States; I know many Negroes. I was a warm admirer of Martin Luther King, but Negroes are not like Americans. If Negroes and Americans live in the same area and under the same circumstances then there is always more criminality among the Negroes. They are a different race.

"Children are made in the same way everywhere on earth, but the children are different. This is not a religious belief, I have never spoken with God. I don't believe in science. I don't believe in books. How could I believe in books? They're all wrong. There's nothing that can replace long experience, having seen what you're talking about yourself. China invaded India. They were stronger than we. How could we have started the war by invading or provoking the

Chinese? What would we have gained by it? Of course they say something else in China. But I know the Chinese. I know how we suffered here in India, how the people suffered. No one can be more sensitive than I. I know even though I wasn't there, I know because I am an Indian. You weren't there. You read books, but how can you believe in books? I don't believe in books and science and facts. The Chinese are a cruel race, I know the Chinese. I certainly think that people can be cruel almost anywhere, but not like the Chinese. In Vietnam, for example, they kill one another and fight. I am not for the United States in Vietnam, but they are not as cruel as the Chinese. And the Japanese. Indians are not cruel. We have never speared children on long poles and showed them to people. I don't believe those kinds of stories about India. Indians would never do such things. We are a superior race in many respects."

His well-manicured hands gesticulate eagerly and confidently. He pours whiskey in the glasses now and then, loosens his tie, opens the collar of his dazzling white shirt, takes off his shoes, and has his slippers brought in. He is very tall for an Indian, about six two, with grayish-white sideburns, a bald pate, black eyeglasses, and a self-conscious, sometimes humorous, look. His manner is relaxed, calm and authoritative with an air of absolute naturalness.

We are sitting on a veranda surrounded by tropical plants, servants and cheese sandwiches; the veranda is part of the mansion he lives in. He is Madras's foremost industrial leader. Now and then he calls one of the trembling black servants, who, with bent back, expressionless face, and hands behind his back, takes the master's orders—ice, soda, newspapers, telephone reports, pillows, coffee, sandwiches, everything is brought pantingly to the master's table by padding servants, yes master, in the clutches of some frightened and subdued family father in the master's service. Beside the master sits the company's second-in-command, a slightly darker, slightly shorter man in clothing of slightly lower quality. He nods assent to everything his boss says. Occasionally he puts in a word or a short sentence between the boss's opinions. His remarks are consistently brushed aside.

When we leave with the second-in-command, he explodes. He has had to sit quietly for several hours and now he spills over, now his own opinions gush and bubble forth—the same as the boss's but in his own words. He talks about India's uneducated workers until he gets blue in the face, the crimes against law and order, the communists, etc. He talks with a trembling voice about his revered boss, who is so good to the workers. And what admiration beams forth when he himself repeats the story—how this man who is completely self-educated has come up in the world like this, has six thousand employees and is so wealthy. Number two has himself been to college, is educated and has previously been in government administration. "One fine day he came and said: 'I want you. I'll hire you. You will get 100 percent more pay than at this place.' I have never regretted accepting the offer. He's a fine man. He's a good man."

Shiv Sena:
Bombay's fascists

The private army whose development has been most violent is Shiv Sena in Bombay. Shiv Sena was founded in 1966 by its present leader, Bal Thakre, and in the beginning of 1969 was estimated to have three hundred thousand members concentrated mainly in Bombay. This figure includes about fifty thousand in a privately equipped army under Thakre's leadership. Shiv Sena has developed quickly, as is evident from the membership figures, and now has strong support not only from the middle class but also among the workers. The communists' oldest and strongest union was in Bombay, but, according to its leader, S. A. Dange (who is also one of the Communist party's leaders), the union has been completely crushed by Shiv Sena.

Shiv Sena exploits and provokes antagonisms between people with different languages. Its slogan is "Maharashtra for the Maharashtrians" (Maharashtra is the state in which Bombay is located). Its posters can be seen in the city: "Warning. You who are not from Bombay, if you have not left the city before the first of October you will be killed the second of October at one o'clock. Take this seriously. Shiv Sena." Shiv Sena showed that these are not merely empty threats in February 1969, when the biggest riot in the city's history began. For several days Shiv Sena had Bombay practically defenseless in its hands. All normal life was paralyzed and the police could not, and apparently did not want to, organize any counterattack before Shiv Sena itself brought an end to the riot. The rioting, directed against southern Indians ("foreigners," as Shiv Sena called them), had by then claimed more than fifty lives, injured two hundred, and destroyed property worth more than twenty million dollars. Those hit hardest were south Indian business owners and hotel owners and south Indian workers. Shiv Sena was also behind the riots in Bhiwandi in 1970 in which five hundred people were killed.

Bombay is one of India's largest industrial centers; close to a third of the country's total industrial investment is there. All the dissatisfaction now fermenting in the city has been channeled against poor southern Indian immigrants, whom

Shiv Sena accuses of taking jobs from "the original Bombay inhabitants." It is typical that Shiv Sena never attacks private industrialists or rich north Indians—these people support Shiv Sena. (According to the latest census, the groups of people against whom Shiv Sena directs its campaign constitute three hundred fifty thousand of the city's more than four million inhabitants—one hundred four thousand Tamil-speaking, ninety-eight thousand Telugu-speaking, sixty-six thousand Malayalam-speaking, and eighty-three thousand Kannada-speaking.) The goal is to stop what is called "the immigration" of these groups and to drive out by violent means those already in the city and the state. In reaction, similar groups have been formed in neighboring states to drive out the Maharashtrians—which may have serious consequences, since there are ten times as many Maharashtrians in these states as there are southern Indians in Bombay.

The ideology of Thakre and Shiv Sena is openly fascistic. Thakre has declared that he has nothing against a dictator, because, he said, "the country needs a Hitler."

"I was educated at Benares University . . ."

"I was educated at Benares University, in engineering. Twenty years ago I said good-bye to everything. I understood that money didn't mean anything, family didn't mean anything—everything like that was meaningless for me. It was my conscience that spoke. Hinduism says that the body is unimportant; it is the soul that is important, it is the soul that will live after death. Since that day twenty years ago, I have lived without pay and without family; I have lived for my calling and have done what I could for the Jan Sangh party.

"This business about India's poverty is very exaggerated. It is something magnified by the West. Of course India is poor, but no famines occur. Bihar? Oh, that business in Bihar—was it last year or the year before, I guess it was last year—that business in Bihar has been exaggerated terribly. Of course there were food shortages—there are people in India who don't eat more than once a day—and that was due to lack of irrigation. That's the biggest problem in India right now. We must do something about that. Did anyone die in Bihar? Ha, that's very exaggerated, like everything said about famine in India; I don't know exactly, I guess maybe a hundred, two hundred. I don't believe the government figures; Jan Sangh has its own figures.

"The important thing is not how much food people have, the important thing is what condition their souls are in. Our party works by direct contact with people; it doesn't matter how long it takes or how many we persuade, the main thing is that we get serious-minded people, people with pure souls. That's how Hinduism works, and I consider it the true religion for the entire human race. Missionaries come to India, Christian missionaries—look what they did in Nagaland, for example. I have nothing against Christians, I just don't want them to come here and destroy our nation. Look at the United States, for example; we have to pay a lot of rupees for the wheat and rice they send here—rupees they spend on their embassies, Peace Corps, etc. But on the other hand they're our friends—England, the USA, France, the free world, since they are democratic countries and we have a common enemy in communism. Communism is our real enemy. Russia and China. The Muslims in India? Oh, it doesn't matter that they're Muslims if it only means that they read the Koran instead of the Gita and go to mosques instead of temples; but when it implies they sympathize with Pakistan! That we can't tolerate!

"The caste system? I can't comment on that. Our party has printed pamphlets and brochures on the subject.

"Class differences, what are they? Oh yes, economic and such—but classes? There are rich and poor in India, of course there are, but the rich help the poor, every wealthy upper-class family in India gives money to the poor, that's no problem.

"The biggest problem in India today is irrigation. That is the main problem. We need land reforms, yes, we must have land reforms. But we can't just take land from those who own it, that can't be done; those who get land must pay for it. How? Yes, in some way one must pay for what one gets from someone else, and if the farmer cannot pay immediately then he must pay after a couple of years when he has the money.

"But more important than all these materialistic questions are the questions about the souls of our people; we must never forget that New Delhi, that what we see outside, is not India. India is something completely different, something one meets only in the countryside, in temples, among yogis, something completely different from this. Factories and such can be found in every land; they are not particularly remarkable, but what is characteristic of India, something quite different, is the idea of and belief in the body's unimportance and the soul's important role, the pure soul."

He has a finely chiseled face, black hair combed back, close-set black eyes, thin dark lips, and a nearly feminine profile. He is very light-skinned, assuredly of high caste. He wears a Swiss watch and a gold ring. He is dressed in a *kurta* white as snow, wide white trousers, and leather sandals in which his feet wriggle and his toes twitch nervously while he speaks. Not only his feet are fidgety; his whole body seems very nervous. He smiles constantly, speaks with a droning, priest-like voice. The whole time he looks out through the window, away from us, with a distant, a very distant, look.

Upper India train

The train to Benares: Allahabad-Benares, third class. We roll on through the landscape, the dry brown landscape; cracked, light, sun-dried earth, dusty little bushes scattered far apart, big spread-out trees. Some of the fields gleam light green but most are naked and dry.

We roll on, surrounded by pilgrims on their way to the holy Ganges with white and red marks on their foreheads and earlobes. Some sleep, some watch us. An old woman sits at the window and sings a sorrowful melody, beating time with her hands on a large sword she is clutching. Sometimes she screams, gesticulates with her arms, pokes them out of the saffron-colored piece of cloth she is covered with from head to foot.

We pass villages; they are the same dull sandy color as the landscape, one scarcely sees them; a few houses have straw roofs, others are just earth. Every inch of the land is used.

People and animals move into the picture. They are silent. The people: the men work in the fields, draw creaking plows with the help of oxen. The women pick the earth, carefully tend every little green plant they see, protect it, clean around it, pray for it. The children herd goats and pigs with sticks in their hands. Dromedaries stride forward with heavy packs, bundles and people on their backs.

We stop at a station. The vendors come up to the windows: tea in clay containers, peanuts, cooked eggs, pocket knives, decorative articles for sale. Beggars come up to us, blind old women and old men, small ragged children with gray eyes.

There is a large mud puddle behind the station, full of water buffalo and people. Everyone there is searching, bending down, everyone is looking for something; for what? The water buffalo move leisurely in the water, gazing around silently. Everything is alive, but even so everything seems completely quiet. A heavy fatigue rests on the land; the people have slept poorly on the cold night ground, most are hungry and sick. They move in slow motion, as if the air were thick dust, difficult to break through. Vultures wait attentively on the treetops, searching ominously for cadavers, sniffing for the stench of corpses, listening for a last sigh.

The platform is full of sleeping human bundles. Every breath they take looks like their last: sick, dim looks, deep coughs, thin limbs and frozen skin, slow movements. There seems to be no border between life and death.

The train rolls on, stops at new stations. At one station two dogs are stuck to one another after intercourse; they stand with their hindquarters together, trying in vain to separate. Two mangy, ugly dogs, skinny and covered with eczema, stuck together. Nobody helps them; a few people laugh at them but most show no concern.

The old woman who was singing gets off the train with a gleaming brass bucket in one hand and the big sword in the other. New passengers climb aboard: two women in white saris, probably widows, with large bundles in their arms. One bundle contains thick, dried grass; it smells like summer. The women's arms are covered with silver rings engraved with animal heads. They sit completely quiet and unmoving. Three small boys have also stepped aboard the train, the oldest with a long bamboo walking stick in his hand. In the middle of the tracks outside our train sleeps a skinny yellow dog, exhausted, unable even to whisk away the flies from his nose. A yard away a crow looks for food among the stones.

A little black man comes into the train, a sweeper; he sweeps under the wooden benches, sweeps away nutshells, orange peels, newspapers and mucus-filled tissues. He swings himself forward on his feet in a squatting position, like an N.

We roll on.

Never a meadow, never a lake, never a forest. Not a single flower. It is dry and brown and every growing thing is covered with dust. The only colorful things to be seen are birds and women's dresses. In one village a score of children sit in the shade of a tree in front of a teacher and read aloud in chorus. Beside them is a field covered with dried cow dung, half-moon-shaped cakes that the low caste gather up for fuel. Here and there piles of cakes have been built up, looking like the large *lingam*s of stone built under the biggest trees in the fields.

The earth gets drier and grayer the farther we go; bushes and trees are less common. Far out in this desolate landscape, people are walking slowly forward, alone or in small groups. Some are lying down, resting themselves, waiting for something; some gather the dry crop or herd animals.

We stop again. There is life and movement, shouting and conversation. Rug vendors walk outside the window; they carry large rolled-up carpets on their heads and skip forward under their loads. Outside our window is a white temple with some dusty lilacs in front. Small children, some with even smaller children on their hips, stand outside and look at the train. What are they thinking?

We roll on. After a quarter of an hour, the train stops on the tracks.

A group of men sit about thirty feet from the railroad tracks preparing breakfast—railway workers let off at their working place, nomads along the rails. Their home: brick upon brick with air between, no mortar, a cloth roof through which the wind howls coldly in the early winter morning. There are seven or eight of them: small, skinny, barefoot, black. Outside their home they have a small fireplace where each turns his own *chapati*; turn and turn the bread on the fire, examine it carefully, turn it a little more and warm stiff hands over the fire before eating breakfast: one cake. They squat on their heels, silent beside one another; a long hard day awaits them on the railroad tracks. A little distance away one of them sits and washes his face and hands in some water he has in a tin container the size of a coffee cup; he washes his throat and neck carefully and rubs the water gently over his face. The water is cold, the air is cold—it is chilly in north India in the winter. No one has anything except a *dhoti*, *kurta* and towel for himself; the towel they wrap on their heads as a turban. A little further away one of them squats and defecates slowly on the ground. Everything is quiet and still; for them eternity passes like this, nomads along the rails. In all probability they have lived here a year. Outside their home grow large red flowers, slightly dirty from the train dust, the only flowers for half a mile around. The men probably break stones during the day. Some fetch big rocks, carry them on their heads to the rails, where others break them into smaller stones while someone breaks them into still smaller ones while someone lays them somewhere on the rails, day after day, world without end, and no one asks why, maybe not even quietly to himself.

We sit in the train in our warm compartment and watch this silent breakfast. We watch it through the window panes

POVERTY

Only one-tenth of India's population consumes more than one rupee's worth of goods per day—about fourteen cents worth—and half the population consumes less than half a rupee's worth per day. Inflation excluded, the situation has been more or less the same since independence.

The poor must spend nearly all their money on food in order to survive, and even then the average intake of calories is below the level necessary for the maintenance of health. The deficiency is even greater if you look at protein consumption.

Development and government aid have not improved the situation of the poor and have not reduced class differences. Inflation and price rises have hit the poor hardest. Taxes are, to an overwhelming extent, indirect, which works to the disadvantage of the poor; not more than one-half of 1 percent of the population pays income tax.

India's democracy is not a democracy for the country's hungry majority. They have no control of their future—that is decided by the few.

A man who is starving, whose tomorrow is dark and uncertain, who cannot read, whose economic life is in the hands of landowners, profiteers, and black marketeers, who cannot, in any real sense, influence the decisions that involve him—such a man is not free. Such a man is subject to lifelong violence. This description applies to the majority of India's populace.

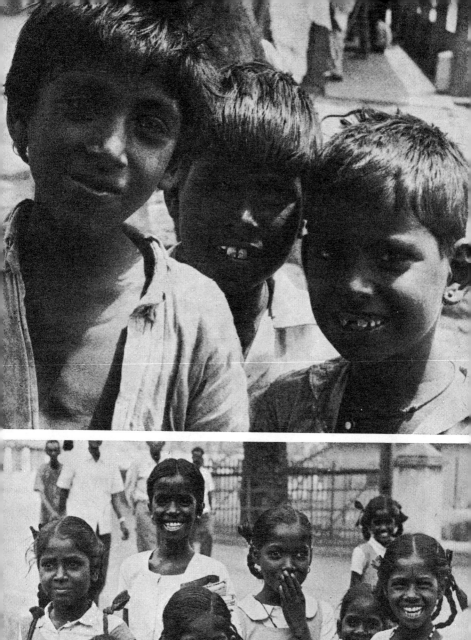

FAMILY PLANNING

The population growth rate has accelerated greatly during the last few decades. This is not because women are giving birth to more children than before, but because more children now survive infancy. An Indian peasant needs perhaps three or four children for there to be someone to take care of him and his wife when they can no longer work. Formerly, he needed seven or eight children for enough to survive, but now nearly all infants live.

Several generations have passed and Indian villagers now understand that their families are unnecessarily large; they want to be able to decide the size of their families themselves.

But in most villages they have heard only vague rumors about family planning, and they often distrust the methods.

But—and this is the really important point—if you ask poor Indians how they would change their situation, they do not usually talk about family planning. This is not because of religion, nor do they think they would be richer if they had smaller families. They talk instead about wanting to have land, cheaper food, and the opportunity to determine their own future.

Family size cannot be considered as an isolated problem. If a poor farming family is small, this does not mean it will be less exploited by merchants, landowners or profiteers. Family planning is important but it will not alter any of the basic relationships that cause such a terrible waste of people and land.

Indians are not poor because of their numbers.

and through an iron grating outside the window pane, put there to keep people from jumping in the train and escaping, just jumping in and leaving everything, leaving their oppressed lives, abandoning everything, refusing to break stones at the railway tracks while every day people travel by in warm compartments, people who surely have shoes on their feet, who eat eggs and toasted bread with butter and tea with milk for breakfast, who have money for train tickets, who see their families, who maybe even enjoy life. A completely different kind of people? They must be.

We sit cramped in third class on wooden benches. Most of our fellow travelers are pilgrims on their way to Benares, the holy city where the Ganges turns toward its source.

Big families; the fathers deal out water from plastic flasks to their tired children, the women sleep with their feet drawn under their saris on the bench.

Holy men sit, with long tangled hair, necklaces, yellow cloths around their hips, long staffs in their hands and red and gray dabs of color symmetrically placed on their faces and arms and legs.

Men and women chew *pan*; their lips shine red and they spit on the floor; the spittle looks like blood.

The whole time some sit and blend their own spice on a leaf; they take a can or newspaper out of the folds of their clothing and carefully lay out its contents: small red pills, small brown kernels, silver-colored grains, yellow powder, black kernels and a dab of white cream put on the leaf which is then folded up into a little package and popped into the mouth. A man sitting next to us asks if we want a taste. He tells us that he teaches chemistry at Benares University.

"But the university is closed now. The communist students are causing trouble. The communists are responsible for the situation in India today. They think only about material things. You believe of course that India is poor, but it is not true. That is communist propaganda that they spread to Europe. The problem in India is that we have forgotten our *dharma*, we have forgotten our religious duties. We ought to think more about the soul's freedom. The communists talk only of money."

He leans close to us and lowers his voice.

"You understand, the communists, they don't believe in God. And the Muslims, we have never been able to trust them. What we must do is think about our souls. It is only by returning to religion, to Hinduism, that we can regain our greatness."

The train stops. Benares. A sea of sound: the songs, flute music and drumbeat of a funeral procession, the rickshaws jingling, holy men mumbling prayers, the tramping of holy cows, car horns, goats, pigs, monkeys, birds, and people, lots of people. The city is full of temples—Shiva temples, Kali temples, Vishnu temples—full of narrow alleyways, full of small cramped shops selling cans with holy color to put on the forehead, cans with holy water from the Ganges, cans with small pills and grains and kernels in various colors, small *lingam* statues, begging bowls for gurus, necklaces made of Shiva's holy flesh, saffron yellow pieces of cloth with Gita texts printed in Hindi.

Many alleys lead down to the Ganges. Here are the holy steps, the bathing huts for women and children, the bathing huts for men, the bathing huts for Muslims, etc. Naked or half-naked people are on their way up or down to the Ganges, where they rinse themselves with the holy water and drink a drop and pray long prayers—or just cool their hot, dusty bodies. Many are old, dry and wrinkled with gray eyes; they have come here to take their last bath and drink their last drop—blessed is he who is cremated at the Ganges beach and then, as ashes, is strewn in the holy river. The bier burns at the beach; it is dusk and the air is sultry.

This is a melting pot of religions, a place of pilgrimage, and home for half a million Indians who live their daily lives here.

Dipak Malik, student at Benares University

"Benares is a sick city. Look around you. There is a dangerous religious fanaticism here; there are plenty of fascist elements. Take our university, for example: this is the center of Hinduism; the university is called the Benares Hindu University. The administrators are RSS supporters. RSS is a Hindu fanatic organization.

"There are special buildings for RSS students on the university campus. They are trained here; they are indoctrinated in fascist ideology; they learn that Hindus are always good and that their enemies are Muslims and communists.

"What this means for us radical students you can well imagine—there is open war at the university. And not only here; the whole city is seething.

"RSS recruits its supporters as early as the primary school years. Schoolboys get a comprehensive education at RSS's own evening schools. Their loyalty is transferred from the family to the organization, which becomes the only anchor point of their existence. The RSS boys stick together in school and this of course continues on up to the university level.

"They try to keep the organization's hierarchy secret; no orders are written down. The members may not question orders from above; obedience is total.

"Our university has been closed several months now. When the fighting reached its peak it was apparent—as was expected—that the police were completely on the RSS students' side. In such a situation one must be strong in order to be able to fight for justice and equality, to fight against the growing fascism."

Jan Sangh and RSS: Hindu fanaticism

Since the Hindus are the single largest group in India, the Hindu fanatic groups now operating in the country constitute the greatest potential danger. At the head of these groups stands the Jan Sangh political party. The party made strong gains in the 1967 election and became the largest opposition party. (It was passed in the 1971 election, however, by the Congress Party (R) with 3 percent of the vote.) Particularly in northern India, Hinduism's domain, Jan Sangh's communalism caught on with the voters: the party's demand that Hindi be the national language would greatly benefit Hindi-speaking northern India.

The party blossomed in 1962, after the war with China. Hatred and fear of China was exploited and enlarged, and the party promoted militant anticommunism against domestic communists. The Communist party was split by the attacks, and its gains of recent years were turned into stagnation and defeat. Jan Sangh has exploited the war with Pakistan and the resulting tension between the two countries in the same way, in a hate campaign against "the country's enemies."

Jan Sangh paints a picture of India's Muslims as Pakistani agents determined to undermine the Indian nation. Fear of the Muslims is stirred up, and they, together with foreign powers and communists, are made scapegoats for everything wrong in India. This is an attempt to disguise the great class differences and growing class antagonisms by creating antagonisms between vertically constructed groups—in north India, religious groups. The English used the same technique during their reign as colonial lords; from the beginning small religious conflicts were fomented in order to prevent a revolt against the colonial regime.

The party plays upon the frustrated feelings of the poor middle class by promising a grandiose Indian foreign policy designed to give India its "proper place" in the world. One plank of this foreign policy is the "liberation" of Tibet, Sinkiang, and Outer and Inner Mongolia, and the reclamation of those areas the party considers lost to Pakistan and China—this to be achieved by an India with an army of a million men and its own nuclear weapons.

Jan Sangh is, however, only the parliamentary arm of the paramilitary RSS organization, which is directly responsible for most of the recent communalistic violence. During 1968 and '69, most non-RSS members were purged from Jan Sangh's leadership, and cooperation between the two is now completely open. For example, Jan Sangh's party leader, A. B. Vajpayee, admits that he is a member of RSS and completely sympathizes with that organization.

RSS was established in 1925 but did not come into the limelight until the partition of India in 1947–48. It was behind many of the grisly riots which shook India during those chaotic months and cost the lives of millions of people. RSS was also responsible for Gandhi's murder, which led to the organization's being outlawed for some years. It has now been permitted to come out of hiding.

The RSS slogan is "ONE LAND, ONE PEOPLE"—a slogan well known in Central Europe; in India, according to RSS and Jan Sangh, it means that the Muslims and other minorities must be "nationalized." One can get an idea of what this means from a statement by M. R. Golwalkar—the führer of RSS for twenty-five years—that India has a lot to learn from Hitler's way of solving Germany's problems. He states: "The Hindus are the country's true children and they constitute a nation because they have blood in common. They are a brotherhood, a race with a common origin and common blood." "Only the Hindus have lived here with the conviction that they are the country's children. Here there are Jews, Parsees, Muslims and Christians; all live here. To regard them as the country's children is generous but it isn't the truth." "As for the Muslims, during all these eight hundred to a thousand years they have only acted as our people's enemies." "Unfortunately, our country's constitution has placed the country's children on equal footing with their attackers and given equal rights to all, in the same way that a stupid person might give equal rights to thieves in the house he gives his children, and then divide his wealth equally among them all."

As the goal of India's foreign policy, Golwalkar conceives of a great India stretching from Afghanistan's western border to the Philippines in the east. The founder of the RSS ideology, V. D. Savarkar, does not stop at this: he conceives of a greater India covering the whole world. RSS's fascistic exploitation of group solidarity—a solidarity directed *against* other groups—can stir strong responses in Indian society, whose social structure has, for thousands of years, been the most rigid, most hierarchically constructed social system in the world, with castes as its building blocks. This system already has group solidarities dividing society into watertight compartments. The caste system, which is as strong as ever, is perhaps one of the reasons why riots in India often become so violent and so bestial. Human beings who customarily regard individuals outside their own groups as of another kind have an especially difficult time identifying with other people's suffering. There are also certain elements of violence-worship in Hindu culture, and fascistic elements which have made Hitler's ideas very popular in many places, especially northern India. One often finds several copies of *Mein Kampf* on bookshelves, and many people consider Hitler's solution to Germany's problems to have a great deal to teach India; this is true not only of groups on the right of the political spectrum.

With their ideology stressing the greatness of the past, their militant Hindu racism, anticommunism, aggressive foreign policy, and dreams of a great India, RSS and Jan Sangh have gained a strong hold on the middle class in the northern Indian cities. This urban middle class is strongly motivated politically and has a great deal of political influence. Middle-class people feel very insecure in their daily life and find a vent for their desperation in RSS ideology. For this reason communalistic riots are often directed against the property of competing groups; it is common, for example, for small businesses and street stands belonging to Muslims to be carefully destroyed and burned by competing Hindu business-men. It must be emphasized that the most important under-lying reason for these communalistic clashes, according to studies now available, is not the spontaneous outburst of religious antagonism but the "political forces of the region operating on a specific economic substructure."*

* Ashwini Ray and S. Chakravartty, in *Karamanji Riots, A Political Study.* New Delhi: 1968.

"India must have the bomb": interview with A. B. Vajpayee, leader of Jan Sangh

—What are the reasons behind the tensions between different groups—differences of language, caste, religion and family property, or the economic situation in India?

—There are tensions, but these tensions are a result primarily of the fact that each group wants to make progress and that there isn't enough for everybody. In the American ambassador's words: "We stand before the revolution of rising expectations." Our yields are not sufficient—even though they sometimes have been excellent. When people realize that their desires haven't been fulfilled, they become disillusioned; then language and religious differences can be used to stir up agitation. If there are few jobs and many applicants, then it is easy for a demagogue to say to the young men in Maharashtra: "You aren't getting any jobs because a lot of people have come to Bombay from the south and taken all the jobs, but if all the southerners are thrown out of Bombay there will be lots of jobs." That is demagoguery. We are trying to fight these forces, but the people's desires must be fulfilled. We must create a feeling in the people that they are participating in a great social and economic change. There are tensions because there are forces working to split the country.

—What forces?

—There are communists who don't accept that India is a nation; they say India is a combination of nationalities and that each nationality, at least in theory, must have the right to leave the union. They encourage every separatist movement. They support all divisive forces.

—What does Jan Sangh think about India's caste system?

—We are opposed to the caste system. It served a purpose perhaps when our society was attacked from without.

—How?

—How? It led to group solidarity; those belonging to a particular caste stuck together and, because of the survival instinct, helped one another. But today the caste system has no value, no sense; it must be gotten rid of. Caste barriers are being removed, but the general elections have, in a certain way, strengthened the caste system because there are caste solidarities. A candidate belonging to a particular caste goes to the voters in his caste and says: "Look, I am your representative, vote for me." Sometimes the voters forget that the problems don't have anything to do with caste. Take economic and social development, for example: they have nothing to do with caste, but to a certain extent caste differences have been accentuated by election procedures.

—What about other religious groups in India, like Muslims and Christians?

—They are Indian citizens; they enjoy full privileges; they must fulfill all responsibilities. There is no discrimination in India. A Muslim is now President, and a Muslim leads the Supreme Court. We don't believe in religious discrimination, just as we don't think one should have special privileges because one belongs to a particular religion; there must be neither discrimination nor special benefits.

—If Muslims are not being discriminated against, shouldn't they be represented in the administration in proportion to their part of the population?

—That would be dangerous; it would strengthen the differences. I can understand a religious minority; I can understand a language minority; but a majority and minority based upon religion cannot be tolerated in the political field. Jan Sangh is a minority party but we could become a majority party any time and the Congress party could be reduced to a minority party. But to divide society on religious grounds and believe the divisions valid in all of life's spheres would lead to the kind of unfortunate consequences that caused the establishment of Pakistan.

—The number of communalistic riots has increased during recent years. What is your view of the RSS organization's role in these?

—RSS has nothing to do with these communalistic clashes; it is a cultural organization devoted to organizing Hindus. The Indian government has appointed commissions to investigate these communalistic riots—not a single investigation report has accused RSS.

—You say "to organize Hindus." In what way?

—To organize Hindus so they can play their part, so they can participate in making India great. Take untouchability or the caste system, for example—if these social injustices are to be rooted out, Hindus must stand united. The casteless must be assimilated with the high castes; there must be an organization to carry out this work. Who will make social reforms in Hindu society? When we say that RSS will organize the Hindus, we don't mean organize them against someone else. No, RSS is not anti-Muslim or anti-Christian.

—Do you feel that the Indian government puts too little emphasis on religion and too much on material growth?

—Not exactly religion, but morality. I prefer to express it that way since religion has to do with external ceremonies. The moral aspect has been neglected to a certain degree, but if we don't do well materially, we won't be able to assert ourselves in the world. We must be strong materially, industrially, economically and militarily, but material growth must be balanced—material welfare at the expense of morality will not lead to happiness. There are welfare problems, too. For the moment we face the problems of poverty and economic underdevelopment, but we are certain that this underdevelopment can be done away with and the differences lessened. We shall not ignore life's moral aspects in our attempts to gain material welfare; the growth must be balanced.

—India has one-quarter of the world's cattle. Can they be used to feed the people?

—No; even if we decided to feed the people with cows, they wouldn't accept it; they would die rather than eat cows.

—Are you for persuading the people to—

—No, no, we are not. On this point we respect the people's feelings.

—How should India's border problems be solved, with Pakistan in Kashmir and with China along the northern border?

—We have lost thousands of square miles of Indian territory both to China and to Pakistan and they continue to occupy large parts of our territory. These areas must be liberated by peaceful means if necessary ... by peaceful means if possible, with violence if necessary. We don't want anyone's territory, but we will not permit anyone to take our territory. We must be on our guard because China's and Pakistan's purposes are not good. They have united themselves against India. China and Pakistan have nothing in common. Pakistan is still a member of the Western Alliance, but because of their mutual hatred of India, China and Pakistan have linked arms, and any day now we could be faced with aggression from both. India must be militarily strong; we must guard our borders; we must liberate the territories now occupied by China and Pakistan.

—You say that India must be militarily strong. Does that include atomic weapons?

—Yes it does, it does. India must have the bomb, we cannot be dependent upon international guarantees. The USA guaranteed that arms assistance to Pakistan would not be used against India, but when Pakistan attacked, this guarantee did not stand in their way.

—Can you imagine a situation when you would use the bomb?

—No, we want the bomb as a deterrent, because if we had the bomb China would not dare attack India.

—Then there is no situation in which you would use the atom bomb?

—No no, if we were not attacked then there would be no question of using the bomb; we want to have the bomb as a deterrent to keep China from using the bomb either as extortion or as a direct threat. The bomb is certainly a political weapon. Many goals can be achieved without using the bomb.

—But if India were attacked with conventional weapons, would you then consider using the atom bomb?

—No, we would try to counter with conventional weapons.

—But if that didn't succeed?

—Yes, if that isn't enough then no weapon would be unthinkable. If a country's existence depends on it, every weapon in its arsenal must be used. But I don't think about this kind of war. When China joined the nuclear weapons club, the military balance was upset to China's advantage.

—What is your position on the Vietnam war, and what influence does this war have on politics in India?

—We are not happy about what is happening in Vietnam. I myself have been in Vietnam and I've told our American friends that they are doomed to defeat. If communism is to be stopped, there must be something higher and more noble to offer the people. Democracy can do this; democracy is a superior way to live. The people will not accept communism if they are guaranteed democratic freedom. If there is no feeling of nationalism, it is very difficult to fight communism, and this has not been encouraged in Vietnam. We are sure that the Americans haven't fought to gain territory in Vietnam, but they are involved in a dirty war. We wish to see Vietnam unified, that Vietnam will be neutral. Both America and Russia, and, if possible, China, should guarantee that Vietnam's neutrality will be respected.

—What do you mean by democracy?

—In North Vietnam there is no democracy. They are militarily strong, they have made progress, but they have adopted communism. If we could have instituted real democracy in South Vietnam, given the people freedom to choose their government and manage their own affairs in their own way, and if South Vietnam could have become prosperous by democratic means, then the people could have chosen between the system which has been adopted in North Vietnam and that in South Vietnam.

—What do you mean by democracy?

—Democracy must be political, economic, and social. By political democracy we mean the right to dissent, the right to criticize, the right to change the government by peaceful means. Individual freedom, the individual's value. It is this lifestyle that can challenge communism. The real challenge to communism is democracy. The people of Czechoslovakia, for example, want more freedom, want to get rid of censorship, want to insure themselves the right to have a different opinion. If there is democracy in a country then it is very difficult for communism to survive.

—And economic and social democracy?

—The economic power concentration must end. The gap between rich and poor must be narrowed and every person must be insured a good life. A minimum standard of living must be insured for everyone. All citizens must partake of the economic wealth. That is economic democracy.

—And social?

—Social democracy means that people are not judged according to birth or family possessions; they are judged according to their qualities.

the rightist opposition and the communist party

RSS fascism and its brand of Hindu communalism has also gained a foothold in the countryside through its appeals to religious groups and through Swatantra, a party similar to Jan Sangh. Swatantra is the party of the dissatisfied landowner class and is active in the northern Indian states, where it is a powerful counterpart to Jan Sangh. A merger of the two parties has been discussed. Swatantra is usually described as the "big business" party, with liberalism and private enterprise as its main goals. This is obviously not the whole truth if one studies how the party operates—at least in northern India, it uses frankly communalistic slogans. The big capitalists in India have considerably better control over politics via the Congress parties. Those big businesses that don't support one of the Congress parties (for example, Birla) support Jan Sangh instead. It is symptomatic that Swatantra's leader, N. G. Ranga, and Golwalkar gave the opening speeches at the RSS annual meeting in Nagpur on September 30, 1968.

Before the 1971 elections, Jan Sangh and Swatantra supporters together constituted 18 percent of the electorate, making them overwhelmingly the largest opposition group. Their opposition was meaningful because of the swing to the right of the Congress party during the 1960s and because of the party split in the fall of 1969. The Congress party, which was formed by the national independence movement at the end of the colonial era, has completely dominated politics in India and has been the only party to lead the union government. Under the leadership first of Nehru and then, after the year and a half of L. B. Shastri's prime ministership, of Nehru's daughter Indira Gandhi, the party has consistently lost another 3 to 4 percent of the vote at each election through 1971.

Before the split, the party had a very wide political base, from a reactionary right wing, under the leadership of party president Siddavanahalli Nijalingappa, to a group of leftist socialists. The party included groups corresponding to practically every other party in Indian politics. During the last part of the decade, relations between Indira Gandhi's center-left wing and Nijalingappa's right wing became more and more strained. Prime Minister Gandhi's mutinies against the party bosses—decisions like the one to nationalize the largest domestic banks—led finally to a party split in 1969.

The 1971 elections were seen by many as a sign of sweeping victory for Indira Gandhi's party [Congress (R)]—a tremendous demonstration of the people's confidence and support. This was probably due to the unfortunately widespread bad habit of confusing the number of seats won with voter support. Congress (R) certainly won more than two-thirds of the seats in Parliament's lower house, but this does not constitute overwhelming support for the government—this majority corresponds to 43 percent of the vote, an increase of only 2 percent over the "catastrophic election" of

1967. Since the voter turnout was only 55 percent, this means that Congress (R) had the support of less than one-fourth of the eligible voters.

One must keep in mind that Indian elections, especially in the countryside, are controlled by local bosses, and that the electoral freedom of the peasants is greatly limited by their dependence on the powers-that-be in the countryside. But the government is also dependent on these bosses and the latest election did not show that they mobilized the people to its support.

In party politics, the right-wing groups have been strengthened by the addition of the new opposition Congress party, Congress (O), and their cumulative strength increased in the 1971 election from 18 to 21 percent of the vote. Congress (R)'s main gains came from the two Socialist parties, which were practically wiped out. The Communist party's portion of the vote increased only slightly. That 43 percent of the vote could give over two-thirds of the seats to Congress (R) can be explained by the Indian electoral system. Each member of Parliament is elected individually by majority district vote, a system which strongly favors a large party against a split opposition.

The ruling Congress party, Congress (R), has, since the split, tried to acquire a radical, socialist image. Besides nationalizing the largest domestic banks, it has tried to push through the abolition of the maharajahs' privileges. From the standpoint of the poor peasants, this is of very little significance and will not in any way improve their daily lives.

All Indian parties, except perhaps Swatantra, talk about socialism at great length, but this talk does no more than pay lip service to the dogma of the Nehru era. Whether the split in the Congress party was caused only by personal antagonisms between the Indira Gandhi group and the party bosses (the so-called "syndicate" under the leadership of

Nijalingappa and former finance minister Morarji Desai), or by deeper-rooted ideological causes, government policies in the early 1970s will tell. In the latter case it will not be sufficient to take away some maharajahs' privileges worth a few million dollars a year; the basic evils must be rooted out—the oppression and hampering of production by the rural elite must be broken, the landowners must be taxed sufficiently, land reforms worth more than the paper they are written on must be pushed through, and private money-lending and business must be replaced by a system that makes it possible for the poor majority to emancipate itself.

But even if the government intended to carry out these reforms, which is doubtful, it would still be impossible because the people who support the party belong to the class whose privileges must be stripped away—the local rulers. The only way a government could push through reforms that go against the rulers in the villages would be by having the poor farmworkers, tenants, and middle peasants organize on their side. No genuine attempt to create organizations and mass movements which could threaten the village rulers has ever been made by either Congress party, nor is it likely any will ever be made. Therefore Indira Gandhi and her Congress party will not be able to solve India's problems. Furthermore, all the economic problems which lie behind the recent growth of various communalistic groups will remain unsolved, since the problems of the cities have, in essence, been caused by the influx of problems from the countryside.

Many people in India fear another wave of communalist riots, resulting in a Hindu-fascistic power takeover. This could happen through a collaboration of the rightist parties, the army, and imperialist interests. But such a coup would further increase the regional tensions between Hindi-speaking north India and Tamil-speaking south India, and could finally lead to civil war. These antagonisms would also be aggravated because many of the army recruits are north Indian—like the Sikhs and Gurkhas. A coup by the army would be interpreted in southern India as a northern Indian occupation.

meeting with a party boss:
interview with S. Nijalingappa

We met Siddavanahalli Nijalingappa at his home in New Delhi and talked with him for an afternoon about India's problems and about the problems of the Congress (O) party. He had not yet formed the new Congress party to the right of Indira Gandhi's group, and spoke as the United Congress Party president. A rather unknown celebrity, he was chosen as party leader in 1967. In his home state, Mysore, he was the undisputed leader of the party. He entered the independence movement in the early 1920s and is considered to have a great deal of political experience, but his main advantage when elected party leader was that he was not directly associated with any of the party's feuding factions. He had of course been criticized for being corrupt and for giving his own caste, *Lingayat*, the economically dominant caste in Mysore, too many favors, but this is not uncommon in Indian political life and is not considered a serious taint.

We asked him whether he considered corruption in India to be a hindrance to development.

—This talk of corruption is exaggerated; it is discussed more than necessary. There is corruption everywhere, in

107

every country; it is in politics, in our daily lives. But I think we talk about it too much; the less we talk about it the better I feel. Of course there is corruption, but it can be explained by poverty. It is a problem we must get to work on and I believe we shall take care of it, but I don't think it is so bad. Maybe it causes delays in administration sometimes, that's all. I don't think it's such a big thing.

(He was just as honest when explaining the reasons for the decline of the Congress party during the latest elections):

—We've made a lot of mistakes. We got self-righteous because we gave the country independence and freedom. Our contact with the people is no longer so intimate, so lively. The economic level hasn't been raised as much as people expected.

—What has distinguished the economic and political development of India since independence?

—We were a poor country. We have tried to do the best we could with our natural resources. Considering the size of the population, it would be difficult to satisfy all our wishes, but I would like to say that India has managed much better than most other countries during the last twenty years. We are rather proud of ourselves.

—Class differences in India are enormous. How can the poor get more out of development and how can they get more say in politics?

—When it comes to the right to be consulted, we have democracy in this country. I can tell you that despite the low literacy rate and thanks to a long cultural history, the people are fairly intelligent and understand the problems better than most people believe. So there remains nothing to do concerning the people's political schooling.

The important thing is to raise our economic level. To lay the foundation for this we have tried to raise the literacy rate, and I am glad to say that the literacy rate has been raised from 20 to 40 percent. We believe we will wipe out illiteracy within fifteen to twenty years, but most important is to put an end to poverty in this country, and that is also feasible. We will take care of all our problems. Agricultural production has gone up, but the population explosion is very great—we increase by more than one Australia per year. But that we can manage too. We've made a breakthrough in agricultural production; within three to four years we will be able to produce all the food we need.

—Where should the balance between industry and agriculture lie in development planning?

—The emphasis must now be laid on agriculture; we must become self-sufficient. Agriculture not only gives us food but also half of all the raw material for industry. Industry then follows automatically.

—How have the attempted land reforms turned out?

—I'm not especially happy about the way the land reforms have worked out in practice. Every state has its own agricultural laws, so they are enormously complicated. The land reforms are making slow progress but will be carried out.

—How will they be carried out? How will the land reforms be made effective? Can you give us any concrete examples?

—They must be carried out more honestly, more forcefully.

—How can the farmers be mobilized and organized politically?

—As I said, our people are pretty well informed politically. This is a democracy, so there are many parties that work among the people and give them political training. We believe in democracy and in the political nurturing of the people.

—Then you think the poor peasants participate enough in India's political life?

—Oh yes! I can tell you that the peasants are perhaps poor but they are very well informed.

—You say you believe in democracy. What do you mean by democracy?

—Democracy is much too old an institution to define. It is rule by the people for the people. The people themselves choose their government.

—You say nothing about economic democracy.

—Economic democracy is a very vague expression. The economy can be developed both under democracy and dictatorship, but in a democracy the citizens cooperate in the work of building up the economy and the citizens themselves decide what sort of economy is best. A democracy respects the individual—communism doesn't.

—What is behind the great group antagonisms found in today's India? How can national unity be strengthened?

—National unity is growing. India is such a large country that it is natural that there are many different languages, but we have practically solved this problem by dividing the country into states according to language barriers. There are still tensions here and there but they are inconsiderable and continually decreasing.

Religion plays an important role, of course. It determines one's sentiments, but as the level of education increases, religion plays a smaller and smaller role in creating tensions.

In a country as large as this, there are antagonisms between religions, languages, castes, and regions. But I want to tell you that, despite this, we are building up the country and the feeling of unity is growing. Of course, it takes time, but we hope to manage it.

—How will the Kashmir question be solved?

—There is nothing to discuss—we have decided it once and for all. Kashmir's people decided several years ago that they want to belong to India. It is a part of India and it will continue to be. There is nothing to discuss, regardless of what people say.

When it comes to our foreign policy, we have remained neutral. I believe it is good to have a third power in the world; I think that India, by not joining any bloc, can make the world's political thinking a little saner. Nehru laid the ground rules for our foreign policy and we follow them. They are good.

—What do you think about the Vietnam war and does it have any effect on India?

—The war as such doesn't really have any direct effect on us. But we have thought about it and we are extremely saddened by the events in Vietnam. We have pleaded for peace, that the bombing end, but America is a big country, perhaps the richest, and doesn't seem to want to listen.

—Would an American withdrawal from Vietnam have any effect on India?

—No, I don't think so.

—Is there any solution to India's boundary dispute with China?

—The solution is their pull-out—it is the only solution. How could there be any other solution? We thought that China would be kindly disposed toward us, but they attacked us suddenly. We have no quarrel with the Chinese people—it is their government that wants to build up its strength by attacking others. They're trying to create problems everywhere. They must pull out.

—Do you mean completely out of Aksai Chin and Ladakh?
—Yes.

—Do you mean the part of Aksai Chin where they built their road?
—Yes.

—What kind of foreign aid do you want? Is there any risk of foreign influence being attached to it?

—We don't want aid with strings attached, but any aid that can help us to develop is welcome if there are no strings.

—Where does the Congress party get its economic support?

—Mostly from within the party. First and foremost, I want to emphasize that we never turn to other countries; we get money through the support of our people.

—What will happen in India during the next five to ten years?

—We have laid the foundation for a bolstering of the country's economy, to make the democracy stable. I am certain that democracy will survive in India, but we must build up the country, root out illiteracy, give the people a better standard of living. This is not a small issue; the foundation is laid, but it is not yet visible. Come back in five or ten years and you will find India more prosperous than today. I am an optimist.

"there are a good many of us girls . . ."

"There are a good many of us girls studying political science at the university, but most of us study English and history. I don't know why. It doesn't matter what we study; we come here only to pass the time until we marry—or, more correctly stated, we come here to get a degree which will give us a higher value in order to marry better. If our parents have picked a suitable partner for us, someone we need a better education to be worthy of, then we come to the university to educate ourselves.

"Very few girls really like to study here; most say that it is only to pass the time until their parents have found someone suitable so they can finally marry and begin thinking about cooking, housekeeping and children. The only subject that is different is medicine; girls study medicine usually because they are interested in learning something.

"It is hard to say what I think about this. Here in India it is not like in Europe. We ourselves don't choose who we are going to live with and have children with, and in a way I believe it is best so—we are happier this way. We don't have to go through unhappy love affairs; we fall in love with the man our parents have chosen for us to marry. But there are also marriages for love these days; not all marriages are arranged. But love marriages often end in divorce, while the arranged ones seldom do; it almost never happens. I think it is wrong to have luxurious weddings costing five thousand rupees. I think that is much too much when there are so many poor in our country; a thousand rupees is sufficient. My sister's wedding cost a thousand rupees and we had three hundred guests. She got a little money to set up house with and a little jewelry of course; daddy gave it to her because he loves her and I will get it too; he promised.

"One thing I think is wrong is that we go to the university needlessly. Either we should stop going or we should use our education after getting our degree and work a few years before we marry, or perhaps—I don't know—when we are married, before we have children. But there aren't any jobs for girls. Being a teacher is so boring and a girl can hardly choose any other occupation. A girl can become a doctor only if she doesn't plan on marrying. I don't really know myself what I will do when I get my degree—perhaps I'll work as a teacher for a few years before I marry, but I want to be at home when I have children. It isn't good for small children to be without their mother all day, and there are so many things a woman must do at home: keep the house neat, plan dinners and parties, make sure it is comfortable for the man when he comes home from his job, and keep check on the servants.

"Perhaps I'll get a job when my children grow up, I don't know now, that's far in the future. I still don't know who I'll marry, but I trust my parents. My sister married a Brahman, a civil engineer, who got part of his education in London. Now they have a big house outside of Bombay. I want it to be like that for me. My sister has an M.A. I have one year left, then I'll leave the university and marry."

COMMUNISM
AND
REVOLUTION

interview with student leaders:
Chand Joshi and Thapan Bose

—What role do the students play in Indian politics today?

—[Chand] : The students' influence is nonexistent except in the cities and those areas where there is a developed middle class—for example, Calcutta and, to a certain extent, Kerala. In three-quarters of the states, the student movement has no direct connection with politics or political parties.

—[Thapan] : In Calcutta and Kerala, which are industrially developed and have a large working class, the student leftist movements have greatly reinforced the working-class movements. But take Uttar Pradesh [India's largest state, with eighty million inhabitants] and Punjab, for example, which aren't industrialized—there, politics tend to be right-wing reactionary; it is natural that student politics are rightist-extremist too. In Uttar Pradesh, 75 percent of the student movement is controlled either by SSP [the Samyukta Socialist party—a political party that calls itself social democratic, advances the landowning interest, and favors a strongly chauvinistic foreign policy] or Jan Sangh.

—What is the social background of Indian students?

—[Chand] : The majority come from the middle and upper classes. The working class and the peasants simply can't afford to send their sons to college; less than 1 percent of the students come from such homes.

—What characterizes current Indian student politics?

—[Chand] : Frustrated petty-bourgeois ideas. India's development has been warped; we haven't even succeeded in moving from feudalism to capitalism. We have been unable even to satisfy the needs of the middle class—the middle class which is the backbone of capitalist society, which preserves the system. Students want a society free from contradiction—which is itself a contradiction. They don't want to change the system.

—[Thapan] : The student movement in India is characterized quite simply by its isolationism; it only cares about student questions, and then only on the local level. The same thing can be said about most political movements in this country—the unions, for example. The student movement derives its narrow outlook from the four parties which have the greatest influence among students: the Congress party, Jan Sangh, the Communist party, and SSP.

—[Chand] : The only issues that get student reaction are petty local questions. The classic example is when a policeman hits a student: only then do students and political parties get involved—not if you talk about changing the system.

—[Thapan] : The problem is that the changeover from feudalism to capitalism is still taking place in this country—

—[Chand] : —*isn't* taking place in this country. . . . This is a capitalist system with feudal values.

—[Thapan] : What is going on in this country is a very special collaboration between feudal lords, capitalists, and imperialists. Look at India's foreign policy, for example. To a certain extent it is progressive, but domestic policy is extremely reactionary.

—[Chand] : The foreign policy became anti-imperialist because the fight for Indian independence was anti-imperialist, but domestic policy is 100 percent capitalist—the leading clique is more British than the British themselves.

—[Thapan]: But the anti-imperialism of the early years of independence was followed by a balancing of interests between the feudal lords, capitalists, and imperialists. The progressive ideas of the independence movement just died when the national bourgeoisie took power—and now they are only interested in keeping power. But, obviously, when a great many countries in Asia, Africa, and Latin America are anti-imperialist, the Indian government must hold to the same line. In this society, it is very difficult for the growing middle class to assert itself. Students soon find that they have very little chance of finding jobs after finishing their education.

—[Chand]: If we don't have a structural revolution, the middle class cannot be appeased; in this circumstance is perhaps India's greatest hope. If there is to be any change, it will come from this dissatisfied middle class. The spark will come from the middle class; it is a part of the structure and if this part explodes, then the whole system will explode more easily.

—But if there really is an anti-imperialist tradition here, why are there so few Vietnam demonstrations? When McNamara recently traveled around India, for example, there were no protests anywhere except Calcutta.

—[Chand]: The students here can't see any connection between the Vietnam war and their own daily lives. In the universities, where student politics are dominated by the upper middle class, it is even worse, since this group gains from the Vietnam war. If you were to tell the students that McNamara promised everybody jobs, he would be India's president tomorrow—if the students had their way.

—[Thapan]: Student protest was born in an atmosphere of frustration, and that can be very dangerous. It's not that students don't understand the disparities; they understand everything, but then they say, "So what?" Most of us, especially those who come from the upper middle class, suffer from split personalities. Nearly every Indian of our generation, however progressive he is, has a double standard. Despite the fact that we come from a middle-class background, we bring with us a set of feudal values. A father expects total obedience from his son, whatever his age. The son is brought up this way and when he is sixteen or seventeen years old he's thrown into the artificial freedom of the university environment. In closed environments, like the university, the student gets a taste of freedom and, if a girl, perhaps reads Françoise Sagan . . . she starts to advocate free sex and possibly even manages to develop some of Sagan's complexes. But the whole time, in the back of her head, she has the same ideas about relationships between men and women as her great-grandmother, her grandmother, and her mother had—and quite certainly the same ones her daughter will have.

—How does this "double standard" affect student politics?

—[Thapan] : As I said earlier, the insights are there but there is a lack of opportunity to break out, because if students break out there is no return.

—[Chand] : Students in India are like the astronauts who left their mother ship to float free in space, but then asked to be taken in again. That's what students are like: when they come to the university—they float in space, they flutter about and make all kinds of mechanical motions, and then they say: "Next time we'll conquer the moon, but take us back just this one time," and then they come back to earth and go home to sleep after the demonstration.

—[Thapan] : A large part of the blame for this inability to free ourselves lies with good old patriarchal organizations, like both of India's Communist parties, which have never been anything but social democratic.

—[Chand] : The leadership of both Communist parties consists to a great extent of old feudal lords—they have made the jump from feudalism to communism, but they are still living with ideas from the independence fight of the 1920s. The leaders believe that the good old national bourgeoisie still has a positive function. They are confused by the problems of capitalism. The communists of our generation are different; we have seen what monopoly capitalism means. Our generation's communists are pure poison to the old leaders; we are the young communists who constitute the so-called extreme left, and we will be able to accomplish something because we don't have the old leaders' prejudices.

—Has the 1967 peasant uprising in Naxalbari in West Bengal had any effect on this leftist movement?

—[Chand] : The uprising had a tremendous effect. At the very least it has sharpened the lines and clarified the problems.

—[Thapan] : Yes, that is important, for now the positions have been clarified. Now one must choose. If one looks at the communists' history in India, one finds that they haven't made a clear statement about the nature of the current situation in India since the twenties. That the communists split several years ago into CPI and CPI (M)—(M) means Marxist— is not due to any ideological differences. The Naxalites succeeded in making it clear that India is a half-colonial country where the ruling clique is a compromise between the feudal lords, the bourgeoisie, and the imperialists. They pointed out the contradictions, clarified the nature of the Indian state, and showed that the fight in India must be antifeudal and anti-imperialist. Thus, in the cities we must carry on a fight against imperialism and monopoly capitalism, in the countryside a total struggle against feudalism. Since the feudal empire is the weakest point, it is there that we must strike. The Naxalbari uprising was a turning point for the entire left and has had a great influence on the student movement—despite the attempt by the reactionary press to obscure its character. In all of India there is not a single progressive daily newspaper; they are all financed either by imperialist or monopoly capitalists.

—You say that the driving force behind the student movement today is the frustrated middle class. Doesn't this carry the risk of a fascist reaction?

—[Chand] : Yes, the risk is very great. The only thing that can prevent a fascist development in India is a strong union between the peasants and the workers—but the left in India is too busy with infighting to realize the danger.

—[Thapan] : The danger lies in the fact that the student movement in India rests in the hands of a frustrated middle class which is only interested in issues that touch the individual directly. It is nearly impossible to get them out into the streets to demonstrate about other issues—but they can easily be gotten out by appealing to their nationalism. This is one of the reasons why Jan Sangh is getting a stronger and stronger grip on the students, especially the party's paramilitary support organization, RSS. In Delhi, for example, there is hardly a single boy from ten to sixteen who hasn't participated in the RSS training camps, where they are indoctrinated with the organization's fascist ideas. India's middle class is courted from all sides and its only possibilities for escape are nationalism and religion. Add to this the government's playing up of artificial tensions between us and Pakistan and China. When it comes to Pakistan, only the monopoly capitalists gained by the partition—not the people of India and Pakistan. I simply cannot understand how even the progressive parties in our country can accept the partition on such an absurd basis as religion. This is an indication of how far from reality the Communist parties are.

—[Chand] : They just sit in Parliament, wait for the revolution, and say that law comes first. Communists believe, as Gandhi did, that the rich will suddenly become kind—either that or they are romantic idealists who think that the revolution will happen by itself. The reactionaries have a strong influence over the entire educational system; they own lots of institutions. The universities are administered either by them or by the United States.

—How extensive is foreign influence on the universities and how does it work?

—[Chand] : During the fourth five-year plan, the United States, through the Ford Foundation, is to pay 75 percent of the costs of university instruction. The United States has complete control of instructional planning; their so-called experts hold all the key positions. They are trying to gain control of all gifted students by showering money on them in the form of scholarships. For an Indian student, it is hard to say no to a dollar.

—[Thapan] : A teacher from the United States will come and say: "Look here, boys, I've got a project. We're going to study the student movement in India. You find out all about the student leaders—their social background, customs, everything that can be of interest." Or they come with a project to map the telecommunications system in some part of India, or a research project about how long an evacuation would take in the event of war. Take, for example, the enormous research project along the entire Chinese border up to the Himalayas—which, it has been shown, the CIA funded.*

—[Chand] : An Indian student can get three or four hundred rupees a week for a research assignment. How can poor students regard them as anything but gods? The United States tries, first of all, to tie up leftist students with money. I myself have been offered a scholarship to Harvard by a well-known CIA agent at the University of Delhi. I told him

* This project, involving academics from the University of California, was discontinued in 1967 when charges were made that it was funded by the CIA.—ED.

to go to hell and said that when I wanted to prostitute myself I would say so. What would have happened if I had said yes? Everyone would have known that I had taken American money, that I got regular invitations to all the cocktail parties at the U.S. embassy. Everyone would suspect that I was a CIA agent.

—[Thapan] : These days everyone suspects everyone else of being in the CIA. In addition, the U.S. embassy itself has admitted participating in this kind of activity. This is so widely known, and money from the United States is so suspect, that their influence on students now takes other, more painful, forms. This has wounded the national pride of the students, and anti-Americanism is now widespread. From the standpoint of the left, this increased nationalism is also very dangerous. Both in India and Pakistan, pure racism is now spreading—especially among the younger people, ten- to fifteen-year-olds.

Only about 5 percent of the students have to become racist in this way in order for us to be finished, since only 10 percent of the students are politically active. This danger is something the "drawing-room" left in our country hasn't realized. We musn't forget that as long as the whole student movement is based in the middle class, it is more likely that politics will go to the right than to the left.

—Do the leftist movements try to broaden their base by increasing their cooperation with peasants and workers?

—[Chand] : Yes, recently more and more of the so-called Naxalites, the revolutionary communists who grew up in India after the Naxalbari revolt, have left the universities to go out into the villages among the workers to work with them.

—[Thapan] : The Communist party has had a very great influence on the workers' movement for several decades, but even so the unions today are totally apolitical. They can strike for months, endure any persecution, just to make things a little better for themselves. They are completely without political consciousness. They are isolationists.

—What must the strategy of the Indian left be in this situation?

—[Thapan] : We must build up political consciousness as the Naxalites do. We must build up conscious peasant movements. Eighty percent of the population lives in the villages under the feudal system; in such a situation a strong peasant movement is especially important. Among city workers, the lower strata of the middle class and the students must be committed to a total fight against the imperialist and monopoly capitalists. We must not let ourselves be fooled by the hocus-pocus of elections every fifth year. Look at what happened in West Bengal after the latest election: a government dominated by communists came to power. They didn't succeed in pushing through the smallest land reform. This led to the peasant uprising in Naxalbari, after which members of the Communist party who supported the insurrection were expelled from the party.

—[Chand] : Working within the system to destroy it doesn't work. If you do that you have to compromise. Always. The system is controlled by big business and the bourgeoisie. This is something the communists in India haven't understood.

—[Thapan] : It's like the pole vaulter who discovers in the middle of his vault that he doesn't have a pole.

"my name is Kalpana . . ."

"My name is Kalpana. That means fantasy. I come from Chittagong, which is now in East Pakistan, from a so-called aristocratic family. My father was a lawyer. I am fifty-four years old, but I don't feel old.

"When I was seven years old I read an old Indian scripture about a man who tried to build a ladder to heaven. He managed to build a tall ladder, but it didn't reach all the way to heaven. I decided then to finish the ladder; I said to my cousin—we lived in a large family—that when I grew up I would finish building that ladder to heaven.

"Ever since I was very small I planned to be a researcher. But first I wanted to be a freedom fighter; I wanted to free my country from the English, from the alien invaders. As a child I was curious about everything; I wanted to examine everything. I recall, for example, that the servants always talked about ghosts, that we should watch out for ghosts. It was dangerous to go out in the middle of the night without having a bit of iron next to your body; if you had some, ghosts wouldn't take you. I went out into the night, even though I was small, to find out if there were ghosts. And when I came home, I was forced to talk about where I had been, for if you lied you would be fried in oil—so went the saying. When I told what I had done I was punished. I investigated everything and I was always punished.

"I finished high school when I was fourteen years old and went to the university, where I studied mathematics and physics, but when I was only thirteen I joined the liberation movement. My family knew nothing about it, not the whole time I was a member, until I was put in prison by the English when I was nineteen years old.

"I was in the movement this way when I first made ammunition and bombs for those who were fighting. I sneaked into the laboratory every night, dressed in boy's clothes with my long hair pushed up—it reached down to my knees—in a cap. My family didn't find out that I was doing this; I sneaked out when the others were asleep. During the days I studied as usual. Sometimes I had to work in the laboratory for the liberation movement in the evenings, too; when my mother asked me where I was going, I said that I had some experiments to perform in the laboratory for my studies. Everyone believed me. Everyone thought I was a calm and sweet girl; I attended to my studies well; I was best in my class, better than the boys even. My teachers thought that I was a sweet and clever girl. No one imagined that when I occasionally asked to go to the bathroom during a lecture, for example, I was actually going out to meet one of my comrades in the liberation movement to give or get a message.

"One night while sneaking out to headquarters where we were having a meeting, my long hair fell out of the cap. Someone saw it and the suspicion started to grow. It was dangerous; that I knew. But I didn't think anyone suspected me; it was unthinkable that a girl from my family would participate in this kind of political fight. But they traced me down as the only freedom fighter from Chittagong who was studying at the University of Calcutta. I was forced to go underground for a time. I left my family and lived with my comrades. There was only one other girl in the group. I led our group. We made ammunition and fought the English. We

127

succeeded in holding all of Chittagong for seven days.

"I was along on a battle when sixteen of my comrades were killed. We fought with pistols and we had hand grenades; they were the only things that we could carry with us. I shot seven Englishmen that time. I wasn't wounded; I just got a scratch on my leg. It was terrible, but we were forced to shoot; we knew that we killed for a good cause; we knew that we had to kill if India was to get its freedom and the oppression was to cease.

"When I was nineteen years old the English captured me. I got life imprisonment. Two other girls captured at the same time were hanged. They were my comrades, but even so I didn't lose hope that I would come out of prison. I don't know, but in some way nothing has ever seemed impossible to me—it seems as if everything can be done; I can do everything, that was how I thought. They had captured me and imprisoned me for life, but I wasn't dead, they hadn't hanged me; I was alive and that was really everything. I helped my comrades in prison keep their morale up; I said to them: 'We must do what we can. There is no sense in breaking the rules of the prison, then we will never get out of here. We must stick to the regulations; we will be sure to eat well, and read a lot every day.' I was never demoralized; I thought I would be released some day.

"When I was captured my father lost his job. He could never have imagined that I would do what I did, even though I always told him when I was small that I wanted to free my country. 'Yes yes,' he always answered, 'you will do that when you grow up.' But he never believed that I would join the liberation movement.

"When I was in prison, I was told that I must tell what I knew about the movement. I said, If you ask me I will only lie, so there is no sense in trying. It was a good man who was to interrogate me. He respected me. He answered that if I didn't want to talk, I didn't have to. I liked him for that.

"After seven and a half years I was released from prison. That sounds strange perhaps, but I knew the whole time that they would let me go.

"When I was small, I could sit forever and watch the stars and the moon, and I used to sit and look at the shadows under the trees, at the black and the white; the black was right next to the white: right next to where it was light and bright and clear, it was completely black, a big mysterious darkness. It was beautiful, it is beautiful. It fascinated me, the light fascinated me. In Chittagong there was no electricity when I was small, so I liked the light from the star-filled sky.

"Perhaps I'm rationalizing when I try to explain to myself now why I supported the liberation movement; maybe I only think afterwards that it was an idea I had from earliest childhood that I wanted to see my country free, that I wanted to help liberate it. I don't know. I didn't really know what freedom was; I didn't know what the word meant, but I had the feeling that there was freedom, and I wanted there to be freedom for all people—exactly like that ladder to heaven, I wanted everyone to be able to climb up to heaven when they died. When a friend of mine once asked me if I wanted to join a political organization, I didn't know what that meant. I was twelve years old then. I asked if it would help people to be free and my friend answered yes, and then I joined the political organization.

"Since I came from an upper-class family and always got what I needed, I didn't know what poverty was, not really, and I had certainly never felt it. But I had seen it; I had seen poverty in Chittagong, seen how the people suffered and starved. I didn't want people to have to live like that.

"I like the little girl I was; I like the time I was curious about everything and wanted to try everything. In a way I'm a little bit of her now. When I was in China ten years ago I

ECONOMIC DEVELOPMENT

The first five-year plan began in 1951. Three five-year plans have been carried through since then, with worsening results. Where is the "economic and social order based on equal opportunities, social justice, the right of a just wage and a measure of social security for all citizens" that was written in as the basic principle of economic planning? Despite all the talk about socialism and a planned economy, social differences have increased rather than decreased.

The fourth plan was begun in 1969. It will not change any of the basic features of distribution in the economy. Its agricultural policy aims to aid farmers most who produce most; private industry will be given greater leeway. The division of power in the economy will not change radically. All this means that the fruits of any economic development will end up in the hands of those already best off.

But increased equality is a prerequisite for faster growth. Poor health and poor education lead to lower work capability. Through the antisocial use by the rich of their wealth, capital is diverted from production instead of being invested and contributing to the exploitation of India's colossal natural resources. Inequality leads to the distortion of production, with emphasis on luxury consumption instead of on productive capital goods. Inequality brings with it enormous waste because people are underemployed.

It is inequality that hinders development.

INDUSTRY

The ruling Congress party professes socialist ideals, although the concentration of industrial power in the hands of a few private owners is greater than in the industrial states of the West. This concentration has not decreased since independence.

State-owned enterprises have cooperated closely with private concerns. The state has invested mainly in sectors unattractive to private industrialists. State controls and licensing have strengthened private monopolies.

So-called socialism has thus contributed to the increased concentration of wealth and control over social development in the hands of a very few people. This has worsened conditions for the impoverished majority. The liaison between the State and Big Business has become stronger of late.

The vast majority of industry is privately owned. Power is concentrated in the hands of a few business families that have tremendous influence; the most powerful of these are the Tatas and the Birlas. The big industries collaborate among themselves and have decisive power over the major political parties. Using bribes and economic pressure, they influence the administration. They dominate opinion formation through their ownership of most of the large newspapers and movie companies. They are closely allied with the rural rulers. They collaborate with foreign private corporations— and this collaboration is actively supported by the United States with its vast economic resources in the country.

It is decisive that influence of private industry is not exercised with aid to the poor and the fulfillment of their basic needs in mind. Its only goal is to make the greatest possible profits.

India's development shows that the profit motive of private enterprise is not an instrument of support for the needy.

got very enthusiastic. I was invited there for three months by my institute—I am a researcher now—but after two months I couldn't stand it any longer; I had to come home to start to work trying to get the Indians to do like the Chinese. I couldn't stand just looking at what they had accomplished, I felt that I must do something so that we would have it as good as they do."

"in my home village people live very poorly . . ."

"In my home village people live very poorly. They live in mud huts; that is, the women and children live in the huts and the men live with the animals. They have no modern tools for farming; everything is as it was in the Stone Age.

"I have been lucky. I got an education and I am a lawyer now. I am privileged; I don't starve, I have a good job in the city; I have good clothes and I can travel a lot; I speak English, I read books.

"I am a Marxist. I have Marxist literature on my bookshelf. I have read a lot of Marxist literature.

"But how can I do anything? How can I go out to agitate among the peasants in my home village, to organize them, to help them to gain their rights? How could I do it? There is nothing I can do. They would accuse me and criticize me for my privileges; they would criticize me for living as I do, because I have a better life than they do. It would be very dangerous.

"I am a Marxist, but how does that help? It is impossible for me to do anything; they would kill me. My family owns land; they would take it from us, they would kill my whole family and take our land from us. I can't do anything."

The whole time he speaks he nervously fingers Che Guevara's diary, which he has just found in a bookstore. It is an Indian edition.

an Indian communism?

In May 1969, a new Indian Communist party was founded: the Communist Party of India (Marxist-Leninist). India now has three Communist parties: after a long history of infighting, the old Communist party split in two in 1964—into the Communist Party of India—the CPI—and the Communist Party of India (Marxist)—the CPI (M).

What do the different parties stand for, what groups do they represent, why do they have internal disputes, what role do they and can they play in modern India with its immense need of transformation?

The Growth of the Indian Communist Party (CPI)

A movement with a purely socialist ideology could scarcely be found in India before the Russian October Revolution. There had been a Hindu reformation in the 1880s—Ram

Mohan Roy had sought to synthesize the European Enlightenment and the Hinduism of the Upanishads; Vivekananda had stormed against the caste system and had talked vaguely about a utopian socialism; the young Tagore, with his nationalistic anti-imperialism and his ideal of equality, had tried to synthesize the Upanishads and socialism. The Congress movement—the independence movement—in existence as early as 1885, was only a small pressure group of middle-class intellectuals without any contact with the masses until the 1920s.

It was the Russian revolution and its successes that had the decisive ideological influence on the growing Indian strain of communism. This Indian communism was therefore strongly dependent from the beginning on the Soviet Communist Party, the CPSU, and the Comintern. The intermediate link during most of the 1920s was the Indian revolutionary M. N. Roy. The Soviet Union's abandonment of czarist Russia's extraterritorial claims in Afghanistan, Persia and Turkey naturally made a strong impression in British-colonized India. Likewise, the antifeudal Soviet agricultural policy was attractive to large groups of the middle class in the cities. By the middle of the twenties, an embryonic Indian communism had developed within the middle class in some of the larger cities. The principal centers were Bombay (organized by CPI's current chairman, S. A. Dange) and Bengal.

By the '20s, the two strategies between which Indian communism was to swing in such a devastating way had already been formed. One, which can perhaps be called Lenin's strategy for the colonial areas, said that the communists should support bourgeois nationalist movements—in India's case, the Congress movement. This meant that every opportunity to work among the masses should be used—even the bourgeois political organizations—in order to lead the workers, peasants, petty bourgeoisie, and bourgeoisie in an anti-imperialist struggle. Before independence, the CPI more or less followed this line during the years 1924-28, 1935-39, and 1945-47. The other strategy had been formulated by, among others, M. N. Roy, and was primarily anticapitalist. M. N. Roy said, in opposition to Lenin, that the bourgeois nationalist movements in colonial areas were not revolutionary and therefore should not be supported; instead, the Communist party should lead the workers, peasants, and petty bourgeoisie in a revolutionary struggle against domestic capitalism. This strategy had been adopted by the second Comintern Congress in 1920 as a possible alternative to Lenin's colonial thesis; it was followed in India in 1928-34 and 1948-50.

Toward the end of the twenties, the Comintern abandoned the "Leninist" strategy, and Indian communists, who had earlier been ordered to work within the Congress movement, were told to stop supporting the Indian nationalists. During these years, the Congress movement had grown, through the efforts of Gandhi, among others, into a mass movement which now reached far out into the villages, even if it perhaps had not mobilized the poor. The left, represented by men like Nehru, gained greater and greater influence and now led the nationalist movement. It was not until 1928 that mass action became an important weapon in the struggle, through a mass campaign of peasants in Bardoli against taxes, and through a strike wave in 1928-29, in which Bombay's textile workers were the vanguard. Nevertheless, the Comintern's directive was followed by the CPI.

Under these circumstances, the English acted against the communists; thirty-one leading communists were accused of conspiracy and were imprisoned during their trial, which lasted three and a half years, in the little city of Meerut, outside Delhi. This resulted in great progress for the CPI both organizationally and in terms of public opinion. Since the prisoners were treated well in prison, they were able to establish, for the first time, a well-organized party office with contacts between leaders from various parts of the country. They were also allowed almost free access to literature and could therefore deepen their theoretical knowledge. Several completed academic degrees in jail. The entire Congress movement backed the communists in their confrontation with the colonial power, and their defense was led by Nehru himself. They became martyrs. The judgment was handed down in 1933, but the English were forced by all the expressions of sympathy for the accused to shorten the sentences, and before the year's end nearly all were free.

Outside the CPI, various so-called terrorist movements had been built, directed against British colonialism. They were most important in Punjab and Bengal (especially in the city of Chittagong). Many of their members were in prison and there became confirmed communists, often succeeding in converting their fellow prisoners. It is said, for example, that six communists in the big jail for political prisoners on the Andaman Islands enlisted 80 percent of the seven hundred prisoners as CPI members. When they were released at the end of the thirties, as heroes, the CPI enjoyed a big gain.

After the CPI's first "real" party congress in 1934, cooperation with the Congress movement began again, following new directions from the Soviet Communist Party and the Comintern. In 1934, the Congress Socialist Party (CSP) was built as a leftist bloc within the Congress movement. Under the CPI's new general secretary, P. C. Joshi, a close, partly secret, cooperation between the CPI and the CSP developed. The CPI's influence increased very quickly in the CSP, and important regional chapters were completely led by the communists—for example, by E. M. S. Namboodiripad in southern India, by Ramamurthi in Tamil Nadu, and by Sundarayya in Andhra Pradesh.

India's intellectuals (with the exception of Nehru) seem not to have reacted strongly to the growth of world fascism until Japan's large-scale attack on China in 1937–38. The distrust of British propaganda led many to take an irresolute stance toward fascism. Just before the Second World War, for instance, the Bengalese nationalist leader Subhas Bose led a large part of the Congress movement in a "Forward Bloc" which would eventually support Japan and Germany against England. At the outbreak of the war, however, the entire Congress movement and the CPI adopted the same line—against Indian participation in the war.

The years before the war brought a very marked increase in political activity in the country. The Congress party increased its membership from half a million in 1936 to five million in 1939. The great peasant organization All India Kisan Sabha (AIKS), founded in 1936, had grown to eight hundred thousand members in 1939.

From "Imperialist War" to "People's War"

Toward the end of 1939, the CPI took a more militant anti-imperialist position. The communists wanted to use the opportunity provided by war to rid India of the British colonial empire and "transform the imperialist war into a revolutionary war." The World War was characterized as an "imperialist war." In 1940, this leftist strategy became even more emphatic, and included attacks on Gandhi. The English reacted by arresting all the leading communists who hadn't managed to go underground.

Near the end of 1941, pressure was increased on the CPI to change its politics to a more pro-British line. This pressure came partly from the CPSU and partly from the English

Communist party, which has had great influence on the CPI during most of its history. The English communist R. Palme Dutt was particularly influential. When Germany attacked the Soviet Union in December 1941, the CPI's politics changed overnight. True to its unshakable loyalty to the CPSU, it closed ranks behind the Soviet Union and England. The imperialist war now became the "people's war," with everything that the term implied in the way of active support for the colonial lords. The sudden shift was a catastrophe for the CPI, which lost its popularity among the more militant workers and peasants. They had a difficult time understanding why the colonial lords should suddenly be supported just because they had the same enemy as another European country, the Soviet Union. S. L. Singh, an old peasant leader from Bihar, estimates that 90 percent of his one thousand cadres immediately left the party. He explains this by the fact that political consciousness at that time was primarily anti-imperialist rather than a solid socialist conviction.

Confidence in the Indian communists was shattered for a long time afterward, and they were to have a hard time freeing themselves from suspicions of disloyalty.

The imprisoned communists were released in 1942, and all the more prominent Congress movement leaders were jailed that same year when the movement hardened its anti-British line and threatened to begin a big "leave India" campaign. This left the field open for the communists; the CPI was legalized and, in the face of Japanese victories on India's eastern border, was armed by the British. The result was great organizational gains for the CPI, which practically took over the Congress Union and the peasant organization. But this could not hide the CPI's great loss of popularity, especially among the peasants, at the end of the war, nor could it offset the increase of anticommunism. The Congress leaders, on the other hand, were now heroes.

The independence movement ran a tumultuous course after the end of the war. On Soviet advice, the CPI lay low during the two years before independence in 1947. The Soviet leaders do not seem to have foreseen independence and, with the CPSU's careful endorsement of Nehru and the Congress movement, the CPI lagged behind as a kind of "loyal opposition" instead of becoming the driving force.

At independence, what was formerly British India was partitioned into India and Pakistan. Since the start of the 1940s the CPI had developed a thesis of "national" self-determination whereby the future India was seen as a confederation of seventeen independent states based upon various language "nationalities." It was therefore quite natural for the party to support the idea of Pakistan despite the fact that it was doubtful whether partition was in the interest of the poor. In any case, this made it possible for northern India's Hindus to support the party. During 1946 and 1947, two large-scale peasant revolts broke out, led by local communists but ignored by the CPI. The first, the Telengana revolt in the principality of Hyderabad, began in the middle of 1946 as a mass campaign against the land-owners and state administration and grew into a full-blown revolt. At its peak early in 1948, the movement had, according to a secret tally, "sovietized" three thousand villages and taken over and distributed one million acres of land. According to the same source, there were two thousand regular guerrilla soldiers and another ten thousand cadres in these villages. In the struggle against the rulers, two thousand land-owners and policemen were killed, while the guerrillas lost the same number. The other great revolt area was in Bengal, where the peasants, through the Tebhaga movement, attempted to reduce land rental to a third of the crop. Revolts also broke out among the peasant population in Kerala and Thanjavur.

After Independence

In 1947, the Soviet attitude toward Nehru and the Congress movement changed. After direct intervention by Stalin, the CPI was able to take a position in opposition to Nehru. The result was a new catastrophe for the party; the Congress leaders stood, at that time, at the peak of their popularity and the CPI was isolated; they were again branded unpatriotic. There was a great deal of truth in this accusation. Loyalty to the CPSU was great and Stalin was exceptionally popular among the communists. He was a symbol of the pure, true revolutionary; he was Krishna.

Since the beginning of the 1940s, an opposition had begun to grow within the party which was more loyal to Stalin than to the sometimes recalcitrant chairman of the CPI, P. C. Joshi. It was led by such men as Dange, Ranadive and Ajoy Ghose—men who were more militant but who were also completely urban-oriented. (Oddly enough, the gains of the Chinese communists seem not to have made an impression upon any segments of Indian communism.) When the opposition took power in the party, it began great purges in the familiar fashion. Revolution within six months was talked about, despite the lack of any nationwide revolutionary organization and the general distrust of the party in the country.

Ranadive, who became the new leader, managed to strengthen the more liberal opposition within the party and, by his lack of interest in the peasants, to create a new opposition group of peasant leaders, primarily from southern India (especially Andhra Pradesh), which took power in the party for a short time. For several years there was a kind of tottering balance of power between these three groups. The position of the peasant leaders was strengthened somewhat by the outcome of the first general election in 1952, when the

CPI's gains were greatest in those areas where the struggle was most violent. In the two districts in the Telengana area where the revolt had been heaviest before being crushed by the Indian army, the communists won twenty-six of twenty-eight seats in the state parliament and all four district seats in the union parliament; one of the leaders received the most votes of any candidate in all of India—more than Nehru. By the beginning of the fifties, the CPSU had switched back to a pro-Nehru line, and the CPI abandoned its anticapitalist left strategy for an anti-imperialist policy in cooperation with the bourgeoisie.

After the United States began to help India's enemy Pakistan militarily in 1953, the contacts between Nehru and the Soviet leaders became more and more intimate. This co-operation reached something of a climax at the start of 1955, just prior to a by-election in Andhra Pradesh—one of the CPI's greatest strongholds. *Pravda* published a complimentary article about Nehru in which not only his anti-imperialist politics but also his domestic policies were applauded. The article was translated and thousands of copies were dis-tributed in Andhra Pradesh. The election was a sound defeat for the CPI. During 1954 and 1955, various communist heads of state shuttled back and forth to New Delhi. Tito spoke in Parliament the same day that Nehru proclaimed the goal of the Congress party to be a "socialistically patterned society;" Khrushchev and Bulganin made a triumphant tour of India and between two and three million people met them in Calcutta; Chou En-lai proclaimed Indian-Chinese friendship with Nehru. But everyone seemed to have forgotten the CPI's existence and the party stood watching the course of events as a dumbfounded spectator.

Towards the Split

The confusion, demoralization and inner conflicts in the CPI were not reduced by de-Stalinization in the Soviet Union and the invasion of Hungary in 1956. The Kerala faction, under the leadership of E. M. S. Namboodiripad, was bolstered in the 1957 election by large election gains which brought the communists to power in the state. This of course strengthened the CPI's "parliamentary" right wing. It led to an "Indianization" of the communists' policies and to a measure of release from Moscow's choking grip. A new faction grew with its eyes fixed on Peking—strongly urban-oriented and, at base, more Stalinist than Maoist.

The CPI lost more of its character as a homogeneous national party and became instead a coalition of various regional parties whose leaders were supported more on their local base than on national reputation. Contact between headquarters and the local groups was reduced and organizational unity disintegrated.

The Border Dispute with China

Between 1959 and 1962, tension between China and India along their long border in the Himalayas increased continually until the border war broke out in the fall of 1962.

The Chinese-Indian border is undoubtedly one of the vaguest boundaries in existence. It lies entirely in the Himalaya mountains. This area is, in many places, very sparsely populated—often only by nomadic tribes—and has for long periods been controlled neither by China nor India. The border dispute between the two countries has concerned mainly two sections of this boundary.

1. The western sector, which, among other areas, consists

of Ladakh and Aksai Chin, divides the Indian portion of Kashmir from Sinkiang and Tibet on the Chinese side. Here the Indians have demanded about fifteen thousand square miles which now are under Chinese control.

2. In the eastern sector, where the disputed boundary is the so-called McMahon line, running from Bhutan to Burma, the situation is the exact opposite of that in the western sector. Here China has laid claim to about thirty-five thousand square miles under Indian control.

On the basis of old maps, treaties, etc., it appears very difficult to determine clearly to which party disputed areas belong. Since 1959, when the dispute gathered steam, China's position on the border question has been that no valid agreements exist and that the border must therefore be set through negotiations. It can be pointed out that China, during the fifties and sixties, made large concessions in boundary agreements about similar vaguely defined territories in the Himalayas with Afghanistan, Nepal, Pakistan, and Burma. In none of these cases did army disputes occur and negotiations were carried out from existing lines of actual control.

India's position has been that the borders are indisputable and that there has not been anything to negotiate about. Thus, India has insisted upon China's withdrawal from all disputed territories.

What, then, are the histories of these areas and what arguments are there for the positions of both countries?

In the western sector, which is controlled in practice by China, the Indians have demanded about fifteen thousand square miles of land north of the present border. It should be noted, however, that the Indians first made their demand in 1954. Before that, no official Indian or British-Indian map had identified these areas as part of India. The boundary had upon various occasions been declared "undefined" by the Indians, but in 1954 it was suddenly moved a long way north

145

of the de facto boundary and the Indians declared that there was no doubt where the border lay.

Geographically, these territories are part of the Tibetan high plateau. All connecting trails run toward Sinkiang or Tibet. The area, practically speaking, lacks any communication whatsoever with India, and the people are completely Tibetan—culturally, in religion, and in language.

Nothing can be more revealing of how remote these areas are from India than the course of events during the 1950s. In 1954, the Chinese began to build a road in Aksai Chin, which India had unilaterally declared to be its own territory the same year. This road follows the path of the old caravan road from Sinkiang to central Tibet and was completed in 1957. It is remarkable that there was no Indian reaction before 1958. The reason for this silence was given by Nehru in a speech in Lok Sabha (the Indian lower house) on February 23, 1961, when he explained that no one had known about this road construction and no one had suspected anything until in 1957 China published a map showing the new road. Despite this, no protests were made before the following year. It appears that India had not the slightest control over these territories, which had been declared indisputably Indian.

In the eastern sector, India ruled the disputed territory—the so-called Northeast Frontier Agency (NEFA). This area was bounded on the north by the McMahon line—agreeing approximately with the line of actual control between India and China. It was named after the British delegate to the Simla conference in 1914, at which the border was determined behind the back of the Chinese delegate in an agreement between the British and Tibetan delegates. Tibet, which stood under Chinese sovereignty, had no authority to conclude any independent agreements with foreign powers. Alistair Lamb writes in his book *The China-India Border*: "The McMahon line as such was never discussed by the

Chinese at the conference . . . in a sense, it was a British trick since McMahon wanted to get the Assam border settled with the minimum of fuss." The agreement was never accepted by the Chinese government and no Chinese government since has ever recognized this border. Not even Chiang Kai-shek has recognized the McMahon line.

It has now come out that this boundary was not drawn with any respect for the area's history, the line of actual control, or the ethnic situation. McMahon acted mostly according to the watershed principle—a particularly untenable principle in these areas. The area is populated by Mongoloid tribes who speak Tibeto-Burman languages. They are related more closely to the Tibetans and Chinese than to the Indian plainsmen. It must be noted, however, that they are not so isolated from India as the western territories are.

The Indians themselves did not take this boundary seriously in the beginning. In 1917, the official Survey of India showed the border south of the NEFA territory in accordance with Chinese claims. The English maps under colonial rule did not show the McMahon line as the boundary with China either. Nehru ignored the McMahon line in his book *Discovery of India,* in an edition as late at 1951. It was only in the 1954 Survey of India that the McMahon line was first shown as the border between India and China.

All this does not mean that China had an obvious right to all the disputed territories. What it does show is that India's position in the dispute was not so strong that it justified their uncompromising position on border negotiations.

The situation along the border worsened during 1959, especially in the western sector. Skirmishes broke out in Ladakh in the summer and fall. In looking back, it seems clear that India must take the greater part of the blame for this fighting. W. Griffith, who can scarcely be called pro-Chinese, wrote in his book *The Sino-Soviet Rift* in 1964: "In

1959, several months after the Chinese crushed the Tibetan rising, the Indians decided secretly to infiltrate and outflank the Chinese border posts in Ladakh ... In 1960, in spite of an abortive meeting between Nehru and Chou En-lai, the frontier incidents continued, and the Indians established new forward border posts in Ladakh."

The Chinese reaction to these Indian attacks was surprisingly conciliatory. On November 7, 1959, the Chinese government suggested that both sides retire twenty kilometers behind the front line in order to avoid further confrontations and that they begin negotiations on the basis of actual control lines. China offered, in essence, to accept the McMahon line if India would give up its obviously weak claim to the western sector. In this context, it can be pointed out that while the western, "Chinese" sector consisted of sparsely populated, barren mountain land, the eastern, "Indian" sector, more than twice as large, was widely cultivated or forested and comparatively densely populated. The offer shows that China did not wish to start a war with India and, in order to avoid one, was willing to concede a great deal. The Indian government's unconditional refusal of the offer showed that the Indian side did not desire a peaceful solution at all.

India increased military pressure in the western sector during 1960 and 1961. Nehru made no attempt to hide the fact that it was India that was the aggressive party. In a speech in Lok Sabha on June 20, 1962, he said about this activity, "India had opened some new control posts endangering the Chinese posts and it was due largely to movements on our side that the Chinese had also to make movements. It is well known in knowledgeable circles in the world that the position in this area has been changing to our advantage and the Chinese are concerned about it."

India further escalated its war preparations in the summer

of 1962 and increased the pressure along the border. The Chinese, of course, did not sit on their hands during the Indian war preparations, but they still wanted to solve the dispute by peaceful means and on September 13, 1962, the Chinese government repeated its offer of November 1959 and suggested a meeting on October 15.

India refused to negotiate if China did not recognize Indian demands in all sectors.

Indian infiltration increased thereafter along the entire border and, in the eastern sector, Indian troops pushed north of the McMahon line. On October 12, Nehru ordered his troops to remove the Chinese from the disputed territories. War hysteria was whipped up in India and the mass media around the world fulminated about the "Chinese aggression." Two days later, Indian Defense Minister Krishna Menon declared that India would "fight to the last man, to the last weapon." China accused India of repeated infringements of Chinese air space and invited India to shoot down every Chinese airplane that flew over Indian territory.

On October 20, large-scale fighting broke out along the entire border. It now appears that it was the Indians who started this, too. One of the best-informed witnesses is General Maxwell D. Taylor, then chairman of the U.S. Joint Chiefs of Staff, who was asked at a congressional hearing in February 1963 if it really was the Indians who began the military operations. Taylor answered, "They were edging forward in the disputed area; yes, sir." From this point on, the testimony was censored.

After a few days of fighting it was clear that China had gained control of the entire front, and on October 24 Chou En-lai offered peaceful negotiations with India on approximately the same terms as the first proposal in 1959. Nehru rejected this generous proposal the same day. Instead he requested foreign military aid. Help came quickly; the first shipments arrived before the end of the month—primarily from the United States and Great Britain. Nehru later added that the previous summer's Soviet offer to deliver MIG pursuit planes still stood.

On November 15, the Indian defense ministry gave the go-ahead to a large-scale attack in the NEFA territory; the Chinese answered with a counterattack the next day. The Chinese soon beat back Indian resistance and the Indian plains lay undefended in front of them. India's largest oil field lay close to their position. Their victory was total. The world press was swamped with fantasy-filled tales of what the "yellow hordes" would now do. They would of course take the oil field, procure China an outlet to the sea at Calcutta, and invade India as the first step on their way toward a Chinese Asia.

The press had not expected what in fact took place. On November 21, the Chinese government made a dramatic move—it unilaterally proclaimed a cease-fire based on the offer of November 7, 1959. The Chinese then retired twenty kilometers behind the McMahon line and, in the other areas, twenty kilometers behind the actual control lines of 1959. All Indian prisoners and even weapons were returned.

From the beginning, S. A. Dange had led an anti-Chinese wing in the Indian Communist party, but the CPI's official position was more reserved. The West Bengal communists in particular favored the Chinese side. The gap between the Soviet and Chinese parties widened quickly during 1959 and the Chinese line toward Nehru hardened. In 1960, there was open antagonism between the two parties. With Khrushchev's attack on Stalin at the twenty-second CPSU Congress in October 1961, the split became clear—on one side the Moscow-liners, with Dange at the fore, and on the other the Stalinists, led by E. M. S. Namboodiripad and strongly represented in Kerala, West Bengal, and Andhra Pradesh. It is said that a few indignant leaders in Kerala, upon learning that Stalin's remains had been removed from Lenin's side, demanded that they be sent to Kerala, where they would receive worthier treatment.

In connection with the war in 1962, nearly all the leftist faction leaders were arrested and close to a thousand communists were imprisoned. The remaining rightist faction, under the leadership of Dange, closed ranks completely behind Nehru, encouraged by the CPSU's cautious support of Nehru. During the anti-Chinese hysteria whipped up in the country for several months, especially in north India, there was little choice.

The CPI had ceased to function as a homogeneous party and, in 1964, the formal split occurred. A new communist party broke away from the CPI and called itself the Communist Party of India (Marxist)—CPI (M). The CPI's strength now lay in north India and in some of the industrial belts; the party was led by Dange. The CPI (M) was strongest in Kerala (where it was led by E. M. S. Namboodiripad) and West Bengal (led by Jyoti Basu). The two parties were of equal strength in Andhra Pradesh. The communists' mass organizations—peasant organizations, unions, student organizations, etc.—were also split by the severe conflicts.

If, in the beginning, there was somewhat more sympathy for the Chinese Communist party in the CPI (M) than in the CPI, it soon disappeared. Many of the most important leaders in the CPI (M)—Namboodiripad, for example—left the CPI more because of anti-Dange feelings than because of ideological conflicts within so-called international communism. After the Soviet invasion of Czechoslavakia, both Indian communist parties supported the Soviet Union. The CPI (M) has, according to very well-informed sources, now begun to receive economic support from the Soviet Union.

The Communist Peasant Organizations

All-India Kisan Sabha, the communist-led peasant organization founded in 1936, managed only to collect middle peasants and some tenants during the entire postwar period. In an official report to the nineteenth session of the AIKS it was said, "There can be no denying the fact that there has always been a serious lag between the Kisan Sabha organization and the actual requirements of the mass peasant movement in the country, particularly in the postindependence period." During the police repression of India's communists from 1948 to 1952, AIKS was practically eliminated as a national organization. After this period, the CPI did not succeed in attracting farmworkers, nor did it even attempt to any great extent to attract them. There was fear in the party of rubbing the landowners the wrong way. AIKS also had great economic difficulties. Membership fees—its primary source of income—provided in 1954, for example, no more than 4,028 rupees.

The CPI's split in the 1960s had a paralyzing effect on AIKS. In October 1967, AIKS split into a CPI-led and a CPI(M)–led peasant organization.

It appears that AIKS was not used by the CPI for revolutionary activities at any time during independence until the split. It is our impression that after the split, both organizations worked as a limiting factor on the various uprisings and violent actions that took place among the peasant population in India after the Naxalbari rebellion of 1967. Both organizations seem to have functioned primarily as campaign organizations for the communist parties in the general elections. The mass campaigns which have been carried through have been peaceful (including, for example, the widespread occupation of uncultivated land in August 1970) and seem to have attempted more to influence the authorities than to mobilize the peasants for a revolutionary struggle.

These mass campaigns have been radicalized, however, and the widespread land occupation shows that it is not only politically possible but indeed politically necessary for the established left-wing parties to use such tactics if they are not to lose influence among the more revolutionary groups. During the last years of the 1960s, both the CPI and the CPI (M) attempted to increase their influence among the farmworkers by setting up special organizations for them.

These agricultural labor unions often appear to use more radical methods than Kisan Sabha. The strongest of them is the CPI-led Andhra Pradesh Agricultural Labor Union, which claimed to have one hundred ten thousand members by 1968. We met its general secretary, Nandury Prasada Rao, and its president, G. Bapanayya, in Hyderabad in 1969. They maintained that agitation, meetings, etc., which were the main working methods of that area's Kisan Sabha, were not enough to attract farmworkers and make them conscious: "The peasants must be made conscious through their struggle with their daily problems." During 1968, the most common form of this struggle was selective strikes among the farmworkers. "We haven't yet begun to arrange these actions in more districts. We strike in perhaps fifteen to twenty villages at a time, or in just five or six, or, at the very most, sixty villages in one area. It is really true that if pay is raised in ten villages, this affects all the other villages in the area and the struggle spreads." The wage demands are, for example, three rupees in those areas where the current wage is two rupees, and the strikes usually last only a few days.

The strikes led to armed conflicts between farmworkers and landowners. "The conflicts are increasing, the landowners are organizing themselves. They have great power in the Congress and Swatantra parties and the state government, where most members are landowners themselves. They

RELIGION

It is said that religion is one of the greatest stumbling blocks to India's economic development, that religion makes Indians think in a totally different way than Westerners. It is said the poor are so apathetic that they are not interested in change. It is even said that economic development is just a Western idea, that the Indians themselves, because of their religion, are not interested in such things.

The simple truth is that the poor Indians, the villagers, are usually not at all religious in the sense of having a thorough knowledge of Hinduism; nor do they rule their actions by religious precepts if, in their view, these ideas are irrational. They almost never cite religion as an explanation for their daily actions. If asked why they do not revolt, they do not answer that they want to be reborn in a better position; they answer that they are afraid of the landowner or the government or the police.

The powerful use religion as an excuse for their injustices. It is quite natural for a landowner to try to show that the caste system, which secures his place at the apex of the hierarchy, has its basis in religion. But this does not mean that religion excuses the injustices.

When Westerners say that "Indians" reason so strangely and, to them, absurdly, they are talking about middle-class Indians. Middle-class Indians live in two very different cultures and so have a dual system of values. They often think in religious terms while the poor Indians, the farmworkers, tend to use more logical reasoning. Both groups are, of course, equally interested in leading lives fit for human beings.

It is not religion that keeps the poor from living decent lives.

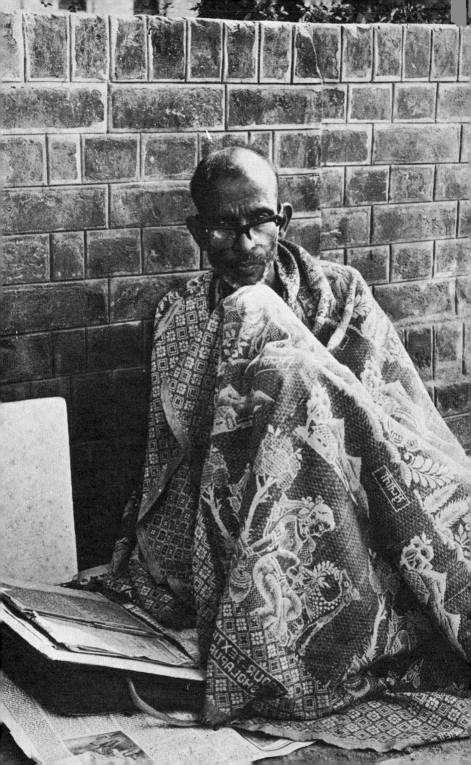

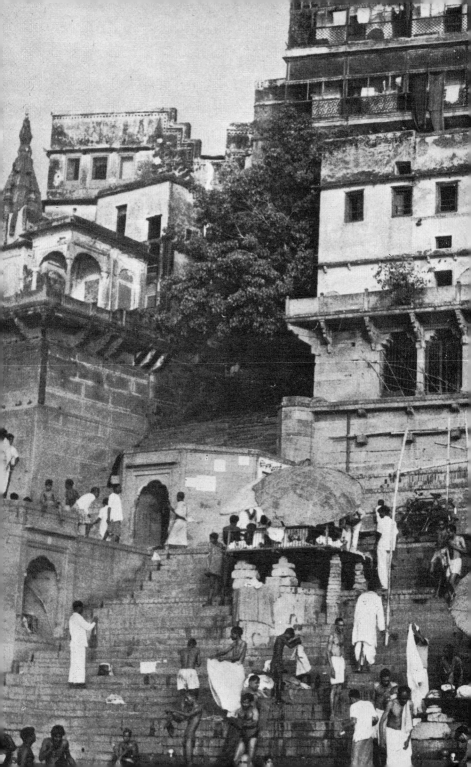

cooperate with the police, hire gangsters, and attack villages, where they plunder and murder."

A Parliamentary Communism?

The CPI (M) usually accuses the CPI of emphasizing parliamentary work too much, but in practice it is difficult to see any differences between the two parties in this respect. In the two states where the communists have dominated the government (Kerala several times since 1957, and West Bengal several times since 1967), it has been the CPI (M) which has been dominant, and this has perhaps increased its interest in parliamentary work. But this interest has been dampened by the success of the Congress party, which has several times taken away the communist lead in the administration. Neither of the two large communist parties has moved toward a coalition with the most extreme right-wing parties, like Jan Sangh, in order to increase its chances of winning posts. Since the 1967 election, the CPI (M) has been more enthusiastic than the CPI in its "anti-Congressism." The current attitudes toward parliamentary work in the parties are confused. On one hand, the possibilities for gaining administrative positions have increased in several of the states through the possibility of coalitions, which can bring worthwhile results in the Indian system of majority elections in single-member constituencies. On the other hand, large groups in both parties realize how little of substance has been achieved in those states where the communists have had parliamentary power (see more about this in the interview with E. M. S. Namboodiripad). Besides, the communists are for the most part as far away as ever from taking a dominant role in the central government. The parties which have increased their power in India as a whole during the last few years are the right-wing parties—Jan Sangh, Swatantra, and now, the opposition Congress party, Congress (O).

PERCENTAGE OF VOTE IN ELECTIONS FOR LOK SABHA,
THE UNION PARLIAMENT

	1952	1957	1962	1967	1971
Jan Sangh, Swatantra and Congress (O)	3	6	14	18	21
CPI and CPI (M)	3	9	10	9	11

Even in states where the communists have come to power, this has occurred not because of any sensational voting gains but rather through coalitions. In the 1967 state parliament election in West Bengal, the two communist parties received 24.5 percent of the vote, while the Congress party got 41.1 percent. In Kerala, on the same occasion, the communists got 32.1 percent against the Congress party's 35.4. (Not included in these figures are the independents who later worked in close cooperation with the respective parties.) But since Indian communists seldom boast about how many voters support them but rather about how many states they have won, an insignificant increase in voter support, such as in West Bengal in 1969 or 1971, is represented as a tremendous victory. In many ways, this is symptomatic of the self-deception of many Indian communists.

A Revolutionary Communism?

During recent years, a rural revolutionary communism has grown up alongside the two communist parties. The peasant revolt in Naxalbari in 1967 had something of a catalytic effect on this movement; there are now groups belonging to the movement in practically every state in India. Despite this, it is still a very small group in relation to the size of the other two communist parties. Its two most important centers lie in West Bengal and in Andhra Pradesh; T. Nagi Reddy, the movement leader with the greatest national reputation, comes from Andhra Pradesh. Up to now, the movement has been most successful among Indian tribesmen in inaccesible mountain areas or jungle areas—both Naxalbari and Srikakulam, another area where the peasants have rebelled, are in such districts. This does not mean, however, that it has not also managed to create vital units in the more heavily populated plains areas: such groups now exist in Bihar and Tamil Nadu.

But even this movement is convulsed by severe antagonisms—primarily between the Andhra Pradesh group and the West Bengal group, led by Kanu Sanyal. T. Nagi Reddy is often described as a Maoist who believes that the people must first be politicized so that they can gradually build up a revolutionary army. A strong party is essential to this task. On the other hand, the Andhra Pradesh group claims that Kanu Sanyal supports a line somewhat closer to Che Guevara's; Sanyal denies it. This line says that the struggle is the first and most important object; by military victories the party wins the peasants to its side. The building of the party can wait.

A discussion of both of these positions need not in itself be negative. In a country as enormous as India there should be room for both—the former, for example, in the highly populated plains areas, where a guerrilla really must be like "a fish in water" and have the population completely on his side if he is to have any chance of success. The discussion would be negative only if it dealt in personalities or, in India's case, in the typical regional antagonisms. The discussion would likewise be a sign of weakness if it implied that, like the earlier Indian communists, one was trying in a blindly idolatrous and automatic way to apply foreign experiences to India in every situation.

When a revolutionary communist party, the CPI (Marxist-Leninist), was founded in May 1969, it was built by Kanu Sanyal and his group, in spite of their earlier opposition toward the founding of a new party. This can be explained as an attempt to exclude T. Nagi Reddy and his revolutionaries by being first.

The important thing about the new revolutionary communist movement which, all things considered, is growing in India today, the thing that divides it from the established communist parties, is that it actively attempts to mobilize the poor peasants and farmworkers, and that in several cases it clearly has brought about solidarity across caste lines.

The Communists Have Not Represented the Poor

Both large communist parties, like other Indian parties, are today and have always been interest groups of, by, and for the upper strata of society. Middle-class intellectuals and wealthy farmers have led the communist movement in the country. Only seldom have workers led the unions. The peasant organizations have, at best, managed to organize the middle peasants and have been led by rich landowners. Their isolation from the impoverished masses and their ties to the Soviet Union have, time after time, led them into the most absurd, or at least the most ambivalent, positions.

In both of the established communist parties today there is something of a generation gap. Many of the main leaders in both parties were already in the front ranks in the 1920s and 1930s.

Indian politics is conducted on several levels and in very different languages. Official politics—politics discussed in the union parliament and also in the state parliament, the politics found in the parties' English-language brochures—mixes ideologies and is played on a pan-Indian field. The political debate in India is carried on in the same terms as the political debate here in the West and has been influenced ideologically chiefly by socialism, Marxism, and liberalism.

Another, more traditional, language has considerably greater meaning in the local political field. There, ideologies play a smaller part, and group interests—caste, religion, language, and, last but not least, finances—are decisive. As long as the communists do not succeed in politicizing the poor, in making them conscious of economic relationships and the power tied to these relationships, and in organizing them, but instead play the game according to the landowners' and profiteers' rules, they will never be more than one party among all the others. They can perhaps, as they have until now, play one landowning caste against another here and there, and thereby come to power in some of India's seventeen states. But as long as they depend on the economic rulers for their power, their ability to make a radical improvement in the situation of the poor will remain a pseudo-power. It seems unrealistic to believe that the communists would even be permitted to exercise this limited power over any large area of India; the triumvirate of landowners–industrial owners– imperialists is much too strong and unified to allow it. Already, leading people in the Congress party have talked about the desirability of outlawing the communist parties.

Political movements which base their strength on the city workers and petty bourgeoisie, like the communists in Calcutta, will perhaps be more able to be militant than "land-owning communists," but they have their own serious weaknesses. This is partly because the Indian crisis is not only an economic crisis but also a cultural, an identity, crisis. The cities, which in India are more consumption-oriented than production-oriented, attract people from the countryside who often do not belong to the poorest strata there. They bring their feudal values, deep-rooted patriarchalism, and a "get-rich-quick" mentality imported from Europe and the United States. These attitudes penetrate far into the rural areas via one of the world's most powerful film industries. Added together, these factors allow the Indian middle and working classes to make their typical swings between extremes—between religious obscurantism and communism, between nihilism and belief in authority, between asceticism and unrestrained greed.

the founder of the communist party: interview with S. A. Dange

Chairman of the Communist party of India organized in the early 1920s in Bombay, one of the country's first communist centers, Dange has been concerned primarily with urban communism and has led the communist union movement since 1945. He belongs to the most Moscow-oriented group in the CPI and is labeled by his opponents in the party as a typical *"apparatchik."*

—How can India's development since independence best be characterized?

—The partition led to serious antagonism between the Hindus and Muslims and Pakistan's invasion of Kashmir led us into a military conflict. Only when the situation calmed down somewhat was it possible for the Congress party under

Nehru's leadership to begin to pursue a more active economic policy.

Politically, this meant, first, to incorporate all the principalities into the Indian union and, second, to create a democratic constitution with the basic rights which had never existed under British rule.

Economically, the Congress party unfortunately was strongly influenced by the capitalists and, to a great extent, also by the landowners. This caused the land reforms to be ineffective. The peasants were not freed of rents, debts, and the remnants of slavery in our country.

The Congress party supported a certain measure of planning in the economy, but the growth of heavy industry was hampered by our dependence on England and the United States. Despite this, some development took place during the first years of independence. The working class grew and began to fight for a better standard of living. Clashes became common between workers and industrialists, between peasants and landowners. Economic development led to increased concentration of ownership.

—Class differences in India today are enormous. How can the poor get a better living standard and how can their power be increased?

—In industry, the three-party conferences which the government set up to regulate industrial-labor relations haven't brought any results. We have a very hard struggle to fight, through strikes and similar methods. The most basic rights have been denied us. We are often shot and imprisoned, but we shall certainly survive.

—What lies behind the antagonisms between religious, language, regional, and caste groups in India?

—They are the legacy of our history. Castes, for example, were introduced in India three thousand years ago. The economy was based upon village crafts and the caste system. This was ended by automation and capitalist production methods. Now, when the economic basis for the caste system has been erased, the positions of the castes have changed but the ideological foundation remains.

It takes a long time to change these old customs. When one considers the language fights, for example, one can see how the various sectors of the bourgeoisie exploit the antagonisms to strengthen their own positions. But we think that these reactionary tendencies are now being replaced by increasing national integration and class solidarity that didn't exist before.

—How does this relate to the growth of a party like Jan Sangh?

—Jan Sangh builds its ideology on worn-out and reactionary Hindu principles and tries to exploit religion to increase its political power. In the same way, Jan Sangh exploits the foreign-policy tension with Pakistan in order to strengthen its grip on the Hindus. The party receives support from the ruling class in the United States and may be a danger in the future for democracy in India.

—What is the relation between agriculture and industry in Indian economic development?

—First and foremost, India is an agricultural country and therefore the emphasis must be placed on industry. Without industrial development, agricultural production cannot grow.

—Why haven't the land reforms been effective and how can they be made effective?

—The laws which were to have put an end to landowner rule promised the landowners economic compensation. The peasants are still paying this compensation. Agriculture cannot be developed because peasants who have economically sound farms don't have any capital, since profits in agriculture are lower than industrial profits, so the banks don't make any loans. All the democratic parties of various hues are now asking for the landowners' rule to be crushed, not only in name but also in practice.

—How can the peasants be mobilized and organized?

—The peasants are now being organized around their need for capital and land. At least half of the money the government gives in aid for fertilizer, etc., is lost through corruption.

—How will you solve the Kashmir problem?

—Kashmir has been part of India for a long time—since 1948. There doesn't have to be any problem as long as Pakistan and certain imperialist powers don't exploit it in order to halt India's development. It can be seen only as a completely internal Indian problem of how the area can be developed on a democratic basis.

—India also has a disputed boundary in the north. How can the border conflict with China be solved and what do you think about the border war of 1962?

—The Indian government has time and again declared itself willing to negotiate with the Chinese to settle the issue, but the Chinese refuse. It is no fault of the Indian government's; there isn't much to do until the Chinese are willing to negotiate. But with their current way of thinking, I don't believe the Chinese want to settle anything with anybody.

—What do you consider to be a just solution to the boundary conflict?

—Nehru maintained that the NEFA area south of the McMahon line is Indian territory; this cannot be arbitrated. The problem is the Ladakh area—in his time Nehru was prepared to give them some sort of control over the area where their road to Sinkiang lies. That ought to be a just solution.

—What kind of foreign aid would you like to see India receive? How do you regard the problem of foreign influence tied to aid?

—In principle we have nothing against foreign aid,

wherever it comes from—the Soviet Union, England, the United States, or anywhere. The question is what kind of conditions are set. Historically, we know that aid from the United States, which is the largest giver, comes with many conditions. Two years ago, for example, they told us to devalue if we wanted to receive aid. The World Bank actually dictated the Indian government's economic policy at that time. They didn't want India to develop any heavy industry, either; they wanted us to be in the same condition as we were under the English. There are a lot of political conditions, besides. Aid from the socialist countries, however, is given without any conditions—and I don't say this because I am a communist. It is a fact.

—How is your party financed?

—Our finances are based upon collections; we have quite a few contributors. You understand, in this country there is a kind of tradition among the rich that is sometimes a little crazy: Indian kings sometimes gave up their fortunes and went out on long pilgrimages. So there are many rich people in this country who support us, but most important, of course, is the support from our own members. This comes from the working class and the middle class. We get twelve to fourteen million votes in the elections and if each of these voters gives just one rupee a year, that is quite a large budget.

—What means, outside of Parliament, will you use to reach your goals?

—For the time being, we think that we can use the parliamentary system to achieve the democracy we want to have. Non-capitalist development, the abolition of monopoly capitalism, and the transition to socialism can be achieved by parliamentary means, combined of course with the outside struggle, the union struggle, strikes, etc. We believe we shall succeed in this way. Thus, our party constitution says that we shall use parliamentary democracy as the means of achieving our ends, but if that fails ... yes, then a non-parliamentary way must be followed. But that isn't on the agenda for now.

—What do you really mean by socialism and democracy?

—What I mean is that the first phase in India must be the abolition of monopoly capitalism, but not of capitalism as a whole. Second, that the democratic constitution isn't democratic; it can be discarded by the government at any time by decree, so democracy must be strengthened within the existing framework, minus the monopolies. That is the important thing. In this way, socialism will be approached. That is what I mean.

—What do you think will happen in India during the next five to ten years?

—We expect that monopoly capitalism's grip will be broken and that a more progressive and democratic government will be established in the nation and in the states. We expect further development of the worker movement to defend workers' rights and wages, a further development of the peasant movement consisting especially of farmworkers, a stronger economy, and organization and struggle among the intelligentsia. We expect a breakdown of the solid front that exists today in the bourgeoisie in which its wiser portion will go to the left. This ought to culminate in a government in Delhi which can serve the people.

Calcutta

Calcutta. An unreal reality. Are there any other places in the world where everything seems so black and white, where the contrasts stand so naked? Are there other places where the rich satisfy their false needs without embarrassment under the gaze of millions of destitute people who barely survive on a sidewalk? There are. But not on such a grand scale as here; there are so many people here. Calcutta is concentrated and compact and crowded and pressed together and it stinks like rotten boils.

Here you can see children, lots of small children, sitting in long rows at eleven o'clock at night with beggars' cups in their hands. Here people sleep packed like sardines on the sidewalk, close beside one another to keep warm during the winter night. Here there are no cycle rickshaws; the rickshaws here are drawn by human legs: thin, black, stringy legs, small men with sweaty faces; quietly they pad forward through the traffic with their rickshaws behind them, in each of the rickshaws a person who can pay the price.

There is continual rush-hour traffic in this city. Black taxicabs, American luxury cars with fat Indians in silk saris and gold ornaments in the back seat and chauffeurs at the wheel; various models of Indian-made Ambassadors with upper-class gentlemen at the wheel, American cigarettes hanging from the corners of their mouths; Vespas with middle-class Indian drivers in white shirts, their families on the riding boards. The wife sits proud and unconcerned on the side, wrapped in her seven-yard sari with a purse in one hand and one or more infants in her arms. Bicycles, millions of bicycles in a chaotic jumble. Buses that roar forward quickly, stop five seconds at each bus stop; the people with the sharpest elbows get on, most wait for hours at the bus stop. Many throw themselves up onto the back of the bus to get a lift, their lives at stake, clinging fast to the steel ladders on the back of the old English double-deckers. The buses are only one of the many reminders of the colonialists in this place, which is in many ways the most British of all India's cities—in architecture, but also in parts of the population: the upper class and all its old Englishmen who "stayed behind," the old women looking like wrinkled standard lamps, the old roses, Calcutta swarms with them.

The main streets of Calcutta, the business district, are packed with shops with European clothes, radio and camera stores, and luxuriously appointed coffeeshops where fifteen-year-old Indians listen to tunes from the fifties. The boys are long-haired and the girls wear short skirts; they are filthy rich, dressed in expensive satin cloth; they look blasé and sophisticated; they chat over a cup of coffee for forty cents or a glass of whiskey for two dollars. On the stairs of these cafés, beggars sit: old women, old men, women, men, children, the blind, the sick, the hungry, the degraded, the lonely; the eyes are all the same—black, entreating and hate-filled at the same time.

The sidewalks are lined with street vendors on both sides, the stands fill a kind of space where a thousand and one small items are sold, household utensils and clothes and the most completely useless things imported from Hong Kong: pens with pin-up girls on the handles, plastic pinwheels that you

171

spin in the air, eyeglasses with cut-glass lenses—you pick the ones you look best in. The vendors do everything they can to draw the attention of the crowd from their competitors. Some perform, some dress up, some cry out their wares or sing their slogans. It is a competitive life and very crowded; many buy, all look, everyone pokes at everything and everyone lets the vendors demonstrate the pens and playthings. There are also vending stands here along the house walls; they have Bengalese sweets, nuts, cigarettes, Coca-Cola, tea, watches and bananas. Here the vendors sit high up on stools, so high that they look down on their customers; they sit cross-legged, counting coins and weighing cashew nuts.

Street life is intense, so intense that you scarcely notice the giant demonstration lines passing by on the street, crowded, yelling masses, thousands of men and women. Calcutta is a thoroughly politicized city. There is a healthy rage here, a political consciousness and a revolutionary tradition. A freshness right in the middle of this sick atmosphere, a willingness to act that gives hope of something more just, something to end the misery choking almost everyone.

Ananta Majee, West Bengal peasant leader

Crows caw and gray sparrows chirp outside the dirty weather-beaten windows with the dusty green shutters. The sound of car horns comes in from the street, construction workers hammer and pound nearby. A sweeper meanders across the floor and swishes his broom so the dust swirls. It is a dark room, small, with a very high ceiling. Peeling paint on the shelf-covered stone wall, the shelves full of papers and more papers in bundled piles, lots of papers, with dust on them, piles of old documents that grow and grow and that no one looks at again after they have finally come to rest on the shelf. There is more paper in Indian offices than we thought existed. It is dark in the room, full of old, dark cupboards. It stinks of urine: the lavatory door is open. We sit around a table with a newspaper tablecloth; we sit on folding steel chairs in a tight ring and drink tea with buffalo milk, eat boiled eggs with pepper and salt and small sweet cakes. We are sitting here with Kisan Sabha leader Ananta Majee, a small thin man with glasses; a history professor at the University of Calcutta, an old Kisan Sabha warrior, one who has been with them from the beginning, tall and strong. He was an acrobat in his youth, is now seventy-six years old with combed-back gray hair and a face hewn in stone. Next to him sit two eager Kisan Sabha workers, with watchful eyes and quick tongues. All are clad in Bengalese attire: white *dhoti*, a piece of cloth draped beautifully around the legs; a long brown woolen *kurta* on top, stretching to the knees. Since it is winter, some have on woolen vests with neck-high collars. Their feet are in sandals, a strap around the big toe and a strap over the top of the arch.

There is a close, collective atmosphere around the table. There is pathos in these men, with their deep knowledge of the injustices in the villages of Bengal.

"There are approximately eleven million farmworkers in West Bengal today, out of a total population of forty-five million. Their problems are very acute. They work only four or five months of the year; the rest of the year they are unemployed. They get very low wages, wretched housing, miserable health care. They are oppressed and half-starved or starved eight to ten months of the year.

"Another exploited group are the sharecroppers who don't own the land they use, but must pay half of the crop in rent. They make up about one-third of the peasant population. They are completely without rights; they have no right of ownership for the land they use; they can be driven away from the land by the landowners at any time. The only chance they have to borrow money is from the moneylender in the village. This means that they will soon become dependent on him, since he can demand very high interest rates. Often, the interest soon becomes greater than the original sum lent. This leads to the *begar* system, a form of slavery. A borrower who cannot repay the loan is forced to perform all kinds of work for the lender for no, or barely nominal, wages. In August and September, peasants often must borrow for seed. They must pay approximately forty rupees per *maund** for seed, but when they have harvested and have to pay back the loan, they get only seventeen to eighteen rupees per *maund* for the rice. They must therefore borrow one *maund* and must pay back nearly three *maund* plus interest. In this way they are doubly exploited by the moneylender.

"Those land reforms which have been instituted have only been carried through on paper. An upper limit was set, for example, on how much land one could own—twenty-five acres. This meant that the landowners gave their land to all their relatives and friends so that the system continued in the old way. There were other loopholes in the law, too. The laws didn't apply to fruit cultivation, for example. A landowner who had five hundred acres of rice cultivation could plant six mango trees in his rice field and, quite suddenly, he had fruit cultivation.

* Approximately eighty pounds.

"This exploitation of the poor peasants is making the food crisis worse. Twelve percent of the rural population owns 62 percent of the land—the best land. The landowner is also the one who holds back the crop from market to push up the prices. He is also a black marketeer and moneylender. In this way they exploit the poor via food prices both in the countryside and the city, giving no incentive for increased production among the poor farmers. This has led to the quick impoverishment of the peasants. Small landowners who are subject to the same exploitation can leave their land. In West Bengal today the number of landless peasants is increasing tremendously."

Kerala:
communist-led state

Coming to India's southernmost state, Kerala, after traveling around India for several months, is a remarkable experience in many ways. Here, clearly destitute people sit and read newspapers; the literacy rate is double that of the rest of India. We don't attract as much attention here as in many other parts of the country; we are treated, for a change, almost as equals. People seem thoroughly politicized: the taxi drivers spontaneously ask us about the situation in Czechoslovakia or give us critical reviews of the country's leading politicians.

Kerala is a state led by communists—by the CPI (M). It is sometimes said that Kerala is the first place in the world where the communists received power through parliamentary elections. The communists have been the dominating power in the coalition regime since they won the 1967 election, but the Communist party first came to power in 1957, although two years later the administration was overthrown by the central government, by emergency legislation.

Not only attitudes seem different here: nature also differs from India's usual dry, dusty, unending grayish-beige. It is green here and the sea and fresh rivers flow through the landscape; coconut palms cover the thick forests; leafy vegetation covers everything.

Kerala's cascades of green are not wealth, however, and the eyes that don't turn away speak of pride, but not of economic independence. Dry statistics show that Kerala is one of the poorest parts of this poor country. In other words, most people here are poor, though the land and the mountains, the forest and the sea abound with wealth.

Income per person in Kerala is about 15 percent lower than the average for India—a shade darker on misery's gray scale. The population density is one of the highest in the world: in 1969, 1,378 people were counted for every square mile, more than three times as many as the average for the rest of India. Unemployment is the highest in the country— Kerala, with scarcely 4 percent of India's population, has, according to accurate figures, a tenth of India's unemployed.

Half of the valuable cultivated land is used for export production. Kerala is one of the world's largest exporters of commodities like coconut fiber, copra, pepper, ginger, cardamom and cashew nuts. In the sand on the beaches there are rare minerals, and in the mountains bauxite was recently discovered. A third of the area is covered by forests, which yield fine hardwoods for export and produce nearly all of India's rubber. The sea also provides shrimp and canned fish for export—another source of valuable foreign currency. The fact is that Kerala, with twenty million of India's five hundred thirty million inhabitants, produces more than one-tenth of the entire country's exports.

Here perhaps is the reason for some of Kerala's economic problems. All these exports provide the central government in New Delhi with more money to dispose of, just as they provide the large trading houses, industrial owners and plantation owners with good incomes; but they don't provide money for the state government to build a better future for Kerala's poor and they don't automatically provide better incomes for the agricultural laborers and industrial workers who, through their labor, make these exports possible.

Interview with P. Govinda Pillai

We are talking with P. Govinda Pillai in his home in Trivandrum. He is the editor-in-chief of *Deshabhimani*, the newspaper of the ruling Communist party. It is hot in the room and his wife mumbles that they ought to have a fan. She teaches philosophy at the university and is concerned about the students' increased interest in American films and sex. Govinda Pillai discusses Black Power and Jan Myrdal before we turn to India. The whole time students come and go, borrow books, talk about a newly started free university, drink coffee with buffalo milk. We ask Govinda Pillai what opportunities the state government has to help the poor achieve a better life.

—Every time we attempt any radical reforms, we meet opposition within the administration. Both the administration and the court system are led by the Congress party, and before them by the English, and as long as Delhi is ruled by bureaucracy and the Congress party, there isn't much we can do here in Kerala.

—Have the unemployment figures improved during the period of your leadership?

—No, we can't influence that, since industrialization is led by the central government. If for example we wish to start an industry here, we have to apply for a license from the central government. This license is granted only if the industry fits in with their capitalist plans. There are scarcely any industries at all in Kerala, so we have one of the lowest per capita incomes in the whole country. We have a great shortage of food production, a 53 percent shortage.

—Have you in any way succeeded in reducing class differences here in Kerala?

—Not much. But in any case I think we can say that there is no sector of the poor that hasn't gained from our policies. For example, the lowest-paid wage-earners have had their wages raised by 30 percent, but we can't tax the high-income earners since income tax is run by the central government. The only thing we can do is use the machinery of government to ease the struggle of the poor.

—But doesn't the state government have great authority in agricultural policies? At least on paper it can do nearly anything—make land reforms, etc.

—Yes, that's true. We have taken very radical measures when it comes to land reforms. We have passed laws to protect the large part of the population which has less than one-twentieth of an acre of land where they have their huts or their houses, from which they could formerly have been evicted at any time. We have also passed laws which protect the tenants' rights. We determine a just rent, somewhere between one-fifth and one-twentieth of the gross product. We are now legislating so that this rent will also go toward payments on the land—so that the land will gradually pass into the hands of the tenants. We have had to use these kinds of ingenious methods in order to get around the constitutional provisions about the sanctity of private property.

But there is a difficulty in all this that not everyone understands. Of course we are putting an end to exploitation by the landowners; but all the people are subjected to a capitalist market economy. Maybe someone gets an acre of land, but then the value of the crop goes down. Then he must turn to the moneylender. Since even land is a commodity, he is soon deprived of it again.

—In this domain, then, it is possible for the state government to bring about basic, institutional changes?

—Yes, yes, but even if we do, there are all the other limitations left. Agriculture is not the decisive factor in the economy. If the whole power structure of society isn't changed, such reforms will never have any real significance.

—Can't a state government break the power of the moneylenders and merchants?

—It can break the power of the moneylenders to a certain extent, but not that of the merchants.

—How can the political system in India be changed? Can it be changed by parliamentary methods?

—Many of us don't think it can. Recent events in India show that development will not take place smoothly. The latest election, for example, shows that in certain parts of the country an extensive radicalization is taking place, but in other parts the reactionaries are gaining ground. Nor are we so naive that we think that just because we came to power in some states the administration in Delhi will say: "Oh, Ali Baba, you take power because we respect democracy!"

—Are you in agreement with the CPI on this point?

—No, they harbor this illusion. Our views differ when it comes to classifying the government. Besides, they follow Moscow too slavishly, although now they are split on the Czechoslovakia issue. We take Castro's position: despite our strong criticism of the Soviet party, we think there was no other way. We also believe that Moscow drove the Czechs and others along the revisionist path.

—Which foreign Communist parties are closest to your position ideologically?

—Ideologically, emotionally, and even a little organizationally, we are closest to the Vietnamese, the Cuban, and perhaps the North Korean and Japanese parties.

—The North Korean too?

—Yes, although on the Czechoslovakia question they have a different opinion. But we don't wish, as we once did, to have any organizational ties with any other party. Solidarity actions, common actions against world imperialism, etc., we want, but no organizational ties.

—You said before that many of your people don't believe that the power structure in India can be changed by parliamentary methods. What is the difference between these people and the so-called Naxalites?

—If they only said that they didn't believe in parliamentary methods, but recommended armed struggle instead, there wouldn't be anything strange. But it isn't there that our opinions differ. The difference is that they are so happy in their ignorance that they can't separate short-range and long-range goals. They have no strategy, no tactics, no line, no detailed program. All they think about are arms. Not that any of them can hold a rifle. We don't disagree with them when it comes to believing in armed struggle, but they think we can follow the Chinese revolution in detail. By this they mean liberating the villages first and then going into the cities. We think that there may be certain things common to the Indian revolution and the Soviet and Chinese, but India is a backward country; we cannot nationalize private property as the first step in the revolution. We can't go to the Chinese extreme, either. India is a much more industrialized country than prerevolutionary China. Monopoly capitalism is strong here. Look at Bombay, Calcutta, Coimbatore, Madras—they are all strongholds of monopoly capitalism. Only the working class can break their power. The peasants and the intellectuals have a major role to play, but it is the working class which must crush the power of monopoly capitalism with a general political strike in the cities.

Here in India the administration is strong. The police are everywhere; there is hardly any part of the country the military cannot reach in a couple of hours. Guerrilla warfare cannot be carried on and liberated territories cannot be held without the support of the workers in the cities.

We have had an Indian middle class for a long time. Their party, the Congress party, was founded in 1884. They had powerful ideologues like Tilak and Gokhale; they brought in ideas like British liberalism, parliamentary democracy, free enterprise. It was a strong middle class; it led the freedom movement and it took power when India became free and it got stronger. Before the war, for example, Birla and Tata, the two biggest capitalists, had only three hundred million rupees total capital; now they have seven billion! The middle class has gotten stronger and stronger; they have built their cities; they have built their power into the state apparatus; they have their bureaucracy; they have built up their army.

Pockets of resistance in the countryside must be combined with a breakdown of the capitalistic order—something that can only be carried out by the working class in the cities. Otherwise, the revolution will be crushed. Look at Naxalbari, look at Wynad in Kerala, look at Srikakulam—all these revolutionary curiosity shops!

All this can only be achieved by a strong, powerful party with influence in the working class. This doesn't mean we will sit and wait for the judgment day. No, with a sense of urgency we must quickly build up the movement. If we don't do this, the bourgeosie will take the initiative. What is happening now—radicalization in some areas, reaction in others—must lead to a confrontation, perhaps between Hindu religious obscurantism in the north and the revolutionary working classes in Bengal and south India.

—But isn't it tragic that the ones who are increasing their grip on those cities are reactionary organizations like RSS and Shiv Sena?

—Quite right, quite right! But I don't think that it is something to be either worried or happy about. Reaction is growing just because the leftist movement and the danger of revolution is strong. Fascism is growing because the old bourgeois parliamentary democracy can no longer protect the reactionaries. Fascism's growth is a measure of its opponent's growth, the growth and strength of the working class.

—But aren't the reactionary powers strongest where the communists are weakest?

—Yes, of course. Geographically this is true, but not for India as a whole. Look at Shiv Sena, which is primarily an anticommunist organization.

—Aren't you afraid that the fascist movement will get so strong that it will take over the central government?

—The possibility cannot be excluded, but it would not be a coup of the same sort as in Hitler's Germany, with its highly developed capitalism. That was fascism's foundation; capitalism is not so highly developed here. In India, development is very uneven and the economy is backward; the economic tentacles of fascism could never stretch so far. A fascist power takeover is possible, but it could never administer and control all of India. It would perhaps be the signal for total civil war.

—Which side would the army help in such a situation?

—As the army now stands, I think that if there was a powerful people's movement, if the unions were to join forces, if a large movement was present, then we could certainly count upon having a large part of the army with us—but not the higher-ranking officers, of course.

—How would you characterize Congress's agricultural policies and the current situation in the countryside?

—Their alleged program was to give the land to the users and to abolish, with compensation, the landowning hierarchy; but in spite of all the plans, the states have refused to carry out the decisions. Only certain areas have gained anything from these laws—those that were already a little better off. The result has not been that the landless have gotten land, but rather that peasants who used land as tenants but had no written agreement have been evicted. There are a great many loopholes in the laws. The landowner who before only took rent now uses the land himself. He gets a part of the land for himself; the rest is dealt out to the tenants, but for that he gets a large sum of money in compensation. Every landowner after the land reform had a great deal of land and a large sum of money to invest in the land. The reforms are creating a new rural elite with great influence in politics. This class influences even a revolutionary party like our own. Take me, for example, or my wife, or him there. We are all Communists, but we also own land. We belong to the middle class. Among Communist leaders, many are from this educated elite. This is why we say that as long as the party's composition isn't altered, it will never be a real tool for revolution.

There can never be any qualitative change in Indian politics until the farmer, who now has neither land nor political power, stands on his own feet and finds his correct place—if not in the administration, then at least in the left. It is noteworthy that when the finance minister introduced taxes on agricultural incomes in his latest budget, it was the so-called Socialist party, SSP, which opposed them. This demonstrates a contradiction between the monopolies and the rural elite. This is the same rural elite that has the power in this new administration and dominates the village councils—the *panchayat* system, which has the power—despite all the talk about universal voting rights, etc.

Our government here in Kerala is trying to introduce village democracy and many of us believe that everything would be changed by it. Actually, there will be nothing but a democracy for the village rich as long as class oppression exists. The same thing applies to our parliamentary democracy—as long as society is divided into classes, Parliament will remain the instrument of the upper class, except in a few cases.

The only thing the land reforms have changed is the forms of exploitation. It is not true that feudalism has been abandoned and replaced by capitalism; instead we have the old kind of exploitation plus the new kind of exploitation within the old class system.

—You say that this new rural elite represents capitalist agriculture. What do you mean by a capitalist farm?

—By this I mean a big farm where the main part of the work is wage labor. Most large farmers employ wage laborers now and then, for harvesting or sowing, for instance. But the capitalist farmer is primarily dependent on wage labor. In certain places they are also adopting modern machinery like tractors and modern pumps.

—The use of wage labor is clearly a necessary criterion of capitalist agriculture, but is it really enough? Does it mean that earlier forms of exploitation have ceased—exploitation by the triumvirate of landowners, black marketeers and moneylenders? Doesn't the term "capitalist agriculture" imply an element of effective exploitation of the land with improved methods, where the goal is the greatest possible productivity? Has this change really occurred in India except in small areas like Punjab and Thanjavur?

—You are absolutely right. What has happened is that a

new form of exploitation—the direct exploitation of wage laborers—has been added to the old. But otherwise I agree entirely. It is about precisely this point that we disagree with the right-wing communists and reformists.

—In Delhi, many in the administration told us about the green revolution. Would you care to comment on this?

—All this talk about the "green revolution" is nothing but humbug. Not that I want to deny that an increase in agricultural production took place last year. An important reason was that we had a good monsoon that year, another reason was better seed; but most significant was that the price of rice and wheat went up so much that it was more profitable to invest in rice than anything else. The result of course was that the increased production lowered prices. This year, the price has gone down close to 40 percent so next year no one will invest in agriculture. Then production will sink if farmers don't get heavy subsidies, but that can't be continued forever. This contradiction can only be solved by altering the economic system and by scrapping the laws of capitalist economy.

—Is this kind of speculation important for a large sector of the Indian economy?

—Yes, an increased monetization has taken place, reaching far out into the villages, since staple foods have become an object of investment.

—How can the famine in Rajasthan be explained, when, quite nearby, Punjab has record crops?

—It is not famine from lack of food, but from the collapse of the economic system. People don't have money to buy the food that is there, so it is a question of lack of buying power, not of lack of food.

—What effects have the American shipments of the so-called PL 480 wheat had?

—They have lowered our production and increased our

dependence on food from outside India. The large sums of rupees in India under American control have had a serious effect on our economy. They hang like a sort of Sword of Damocles over the Indian economy.

Interview with K. Mathew Kurian

K. Mathew Kurian, state economic adviser and member of the planning commission, talked about the difficulties in carrying out radical changes. He told us that the real power lay in Delhi and that the government in Delhi itself exploited states where Congress party members were not in power.

—What limitations are there on what a state government like Kerala's can carry out? What goals do you have? What has been done?

—This is not a Communist regime but rather a coalition government which includes other members, like Social Democrats, and we must adjust our goals accordingly. We must regard this regime as just one step forward.

Personally, I think that a government like ours has only three reasons for existing. First, in Kerala the Congress party, which represents the state power in India as a whole, lost the election. But this doesn't mean that they have lost power—they are still in Delhi. Now, when the left parties have parliamentary power in small portions of the country like Kerala and West Bengal, we can think of the maintenance of this power as an interim tactic until we get power in Delhi. With this limited power we should accomplish as much as we can for the people who voted us in. Second, we can be a government in opposition—in opposition to the central government. The conflict between central and state government, between the central government's class interest and the class interest we represent, must be intensified. Third, this is a unique opportunity to train a revolutionary party in the handling of routine problems, in administration, etc. All these problems can be extremely intricate.

Concerning the first reason for our existence, I can think of three different aspects of what we can achieve for the class interests that support us. One aspect concerns industry, one agriculture, and the last, administrative reforms and planning in their literal sense. Kerala is one of India's least industrially developed states. Traditionally, all large industries are located in Maharashtra, Gujarat, West Bengal and, to a certain extent, Madras and Punjab. They are the most developed regions and in a capitalist economy the most developed regions tend to develop most quickly. Underdeveloped regions like Kerala tend to continue to be underdeveloped. Above all, Kerala has been neglected for a long time, consciously or unconsciously, by the central government, when we weren't in power.

The industries that we have are primarily traditional industries with poor technology, low wages, and an inability to grow. The state government here could use part of its limited budget resources in helping these areas, where poverty is great and unemployment concentrated. Now, we have noticed that when the workers succeed in getting slightly better contracts for higher wages, the industrial owners often close their factories and farm out production to households in order to escape industrial legislation. This happens in the coconut fiber sector and in the cashew nut industry, two of our largest industrial sectors. In this way the industrial owners have succeeded in lowering wages from sixty rupees a month to eighteen to twenty rupees a month in these industries. We must rejuvenate and modernize this whole traditional industrial sector and we must also develop more modern industries. But here our small resources come in as a limiting factor. Each district ought to have more industry based as much as possible on the district's own resources.

These industries must not be isolated but must be tied to subsidiaries and small industries in the neighboring area. We have thousands of jobless engineers in Kerala who could be employed.

In the agricultural sector the problem is more ticklish. The state government's authority is limited to two areas: land reform legislation and support to small units of less than two acres. These small producers are actually the most productive; their saving habits aren't too bad either—for small units, between 6 and 8 percent saved per year, and for the larger units, 10 to 11 percent. We cannot nationalize the soil, but we can support cooperation between small farmers, bringing them rationalization profits within the system. You mustn't believe, for example, that credit cooperation breaks the power of the moneylenders; on the contrary, we have found that these new institutions are often exploited by the moneylenders. A fairly strong organization among the farmworkers has recently been started, directed primarily against the rich farmers and capitalist farmers here, and I think that we ought to support such a movement.

Then we come to general planning. We were the first state government to set up a planning commission with extensive responsibilities. The commission makes it easier for us to exercise pressure on the central government.

—Have you had any opportunity to reduce economic class differences?

—Class differences in Kerala will continue to increase as long as the present power structure and economic structure stand. The coalition government in Kerala has not in any decisive way changed the state power in Kerala.

—How are you affected by foreign aid?

—Eighteen years of planning in this country has, despite Nehru's talk about a socialist pattern of society, resulted in increased concentration, increased power in the hands of the oligarchs, and increased inequality between states and regions, and between sectors of the population. This is due primarily to the fact that the development process was so heavily based on foreign aid and foreign capital—which further amplified the tendencies toward concentration in the country. Seventy-five big monopolistic families control approximately 46 percent of the country's total industrial capital.

We should not totally reject all kinds of foreign aid, however. The evaluation of the aid must be based on the aid's character—which depends on both who gives it and who takes it. It is not impossible that help from a socialist country could be used by monopolistic enterprise—which thereby further strengthens its position. Aid from the Soviet Union has clearly strengthened the concentration of private capital in India, in cooperation with American capital. When the Soviet Union gave aid to the official sector it was generally believed that this would strengthen the official sector and socialism, but the fact is that the official sector strengthened the private sector instead of itself being strengthened—partly through direct subsidies, especially to export industries, and partly through the distribution of licenses and investment loans which have gone more and more to monopolistic groups. The cycle is completed like this: first the government sets up a large steel sector and builds up its infrastructure, which helps the private sector; then it expands the private sector with loans and subsidies from the official sector and tax money, which is then channeled more and more into the private sector.

—What kind of relationships exist between domestic and foreign capital and between the various kinds of capital within the country?

—It is clear that in certain situations there are inherent contradictions between different sectors of the Indian bourgeoisie, but they are difficult to define in clear terms. Tata and Birla can, for example, sometimes cooperate in pushing through restrictions on foreign capital, but at the same time they can collaborate with foreign capitalists in order to gain certain other benefits. Indian capital can be characterized by collaboration and opportunism, with minor opposition to foreign capital in certain cases. In the same way, one can sometimes see contradictions between small and large capital.

—What has characterized development in the agricultural sector in India and what is happening now?

—After two dry years, we have now had one and a half years of increased agricultural production. The main reason for this is better seed. The weather has also helped.

—Have prices and new production methods had any significance?

—During the drought, prices were in general very high; this stimulated cultivators to use the new seed. Now, since production has increased, the prices have dropped. The lesson to be learned is that, given the existing relations in Indian agriculture, characterized by high concentration of land in a few hands and many small farmers (25 percent own 75 percent of the land) and various kinds of domination through concealed land ownership, the improvements resulting from the introduction of new technology and new seed will not last very long. Today's low prices mean that cultivators can expect low prices in the future, too, and they are afraid to invest in agriculture. I believe, therefore, that the agricultural crisis will continue despite these technological breakthroughs.

—Is it correct to say that Indian agriculture is changing from feudal agriculture to capitalist agriculture?

—These two forms have existed side by side and overlapped one another for a long time. You might even say that when capitalism is strengthened, feudalism is also strengthened. What you see in India today is a collaboration between feudal elements in the countryside, foreign monopoly capital, and growing Indian capital.

"The Father of Kerala":
Interview with E. M. S. Namboodiripad

We meet a porter at a state hotel by the sea outside Trivandrum. Slightly over twenty years old, a broad smile and bright eyes under black bangs. We are standing at the edge of the beach, looking out over the waves of the Indian Ocean, where the fishermen balance on narrow boats, hollowed-out tree trunks. Men and small boys bathe while women and girls watch. The air is humid and the sand is hot.

"Namboodiripad is our father. Some even call him God. We poor have had our lot improved since he became our chief of state, but we have a long way to go."

What English the porter knows he has learned by talking to tourists. He is very relaxed and treats us as equals, not in the same way we have become accustomed to in other parts of India, as superiors. This is something new, and we meet it all the time in Kerala; there is no fawning adulation because we are Europeans.

In the evening we go into Trivandrum to meet "the father of Kerala." We get a ride in a large white car. At the wheel sits a man in a black suit. The porter comes along with us; he has an errand in the city. The man at the wheel asks if we are from the United States—he admires the United States, regards it as a rich country. He doesn't have much use for Kerala's government. They want to take away what you have, he sighs. He owns a construction firm "with many employees."

The porter sits quietly alongside.

Since the thirties, E. M. S. Namboodiripad has been one of the most important figures in Indian communism. Now one of the leaders of the Communist Party of India (Marxist), he had led all the communist state governments in Kerala and was its chief of state when we interviewed him in March 1968. Because of conflicts with "rightist Communists" in the government, the regime toppled in October 1969, with mutual accusations of corruption. "E.M.S." is regarded as one of the more moderate men in the party leadership.

He receives us in his office, a gigantic hall, bare except for a lot of wooden chairs and an enormous desk in one corner. It takes us a while to spot the little man behind all the papers. He is very warm and generates tremendous energy. He talks in detail and at length about the difficulties of Kerala and of India. Namboodiripad has a speech impediment and it is difficult to follow him when he gets worked up; when he starts to talk about imperialism, we can't understand a word.

—What are the primary accomplishments of your government since the last election?

—I want to say from the beginning that a state government under the Indian constitution works under serious limitations. The first limitation is constitutional—the state government's power and functions are strictly limited. The state government has no power over the key sectors of economic activity like industry and trade—for example, over how we may use our own export crops. Because of this and other similar limitations, a state government cannot plan the economy—that's the central government's function. This is one limitation. Another is that even for those functions which, according to the constitution, formally belong to the state government, there are financial limitations. The distribution of funds between the central and state governments is such that all the flexible income sources belong to the central government except the sales tax. All other income sources, like income tax and the customs and excise tax, belong to the central government. All the states, regardless of political hue, are greatly dissatisfied with the workings of this system. Each year they must go to the central government to find out the distribution of funds for the next year; all budget work and planning must take place at the central government level. So we cannot expect a new state government to bring about any basic changes.

Once we have considered this question, we can then ask: Within these limits, what have we done? We are trying to create class consciousness. The people have freedom to organize themselves and to fight for their rights; we have taken away the restrictions which earlier regimes put on this freedom. Our government supports attempts at political struggle and organization. In this way, all the various sectors of the population have succeeded in achieving something—perhaps not always much, but something. Take for example the workers in a certain factory: thanks to their own organized struggle, thanks to the support our government has given them, thanks to our minimal use of police, they have received a minimum raise of seventy rupees a month. This happened in one of Birla's factories. The most important thing we have achieved is to give the people more freedom to organize themselves.

We must remember that this must be part of a struggle on a pan-Indian level. We are not isolated in Kerala; we are a part of India's democratic movement.

—Eighty percent of India's population lives in the countryside. At least on paper, the states have great authority in agricultural policy. Do the states have any opportunities to bring about radical changes in the countryside?

—No. There are two serious limitations. The first is that agriculture is not an isolated sector; the problems of agriculture are related to industrial problems. Modern agriculture doesn't require as many people as it now employs. A reorganization of agriculture along more scientific lines requires that a large part of the population be taken out of agriculture. On the one hand, development of industry lightens the pressure on the land; on the other, it facilitates a technical modernization of agriculture. This is one aspect. Another is that even the little we can do within the limited agricultural sector requires financial resources. If we want to start a large irrigation project, for example, it costs a lot of money; we can't do it without the cooperation of the central government.

When it comes to economics, we note that the states have a shortage of funds. Our own budget shows a deficit of approximately two hundred million rupees. The central government also shows a deficit, but there is a difference. They can cover their deficit by printing more bank notes.

The same thing goes for education. Formally, we can do nearly anything with our educational system, but the question of resources comes in again.

—Is it impossible, because of these restrictions, for a state government to crush the power of the countryside's triumvirate—landowner, merchant, moneylender?

—The state cannot do it alone. Our party is clearly divided from the other parties. We want to use all the power we have, but we must continue to explain to the people that their salvation lies only in a basic change in the whole country, because the leviathan is there; he is sitting on us.

—How are your relations with the CPI? What are the most important differences between you?

—It is difficult to catalogue all the differences in a short time, but I can say that as far as we are concerned, we rule ourselves by strict Marxist theory about the state and revolution. At the same time, we think that if we make the greatest possible use of the constitutional opportunities that development can give, we won't fall for the illusion, or create illusions among the people, that we can change the system through constitutional activity. When you get right down to it, Marx and especially Lenin emphasize the fact that bourgeois democracy is just a special kind of bourgeois dictatorship. Whenever the ruling classes see that the working class is using this bourgeois democratic system to further its class interests in order to weaken and defeat the ruling class, they throw away their democratic masks and show their true faces. We harbor no illusions that we can in this way carry out a basic social revolution.

The rightist Communists are of a different opinion. They talk about what they call structural reforms, by which they think fundamental social changes will gradually be achieved.

—How can modern Indian society be characterized?

—We think that the state in India is a tool of the bourgeois class in alliance with the landowners, under the leadership of the wealthy bourgeoisie in collaboration with foreign monopolists.

—Does the CPI have a different opinion about this?

—They have altered their position slightly. In their original program, they said that this is the state of the bourgeoisie, the whole bourgeoisie. This means that it is not the unified organ of the bourgeoisie and the landowners. They thus deny the fact that it is led by the wealthy bourgeoisie. They also deny the significance of the collaboration between Indian big business and foreign monopolies. Under the pressure of development they have been forced to make small changes, but as a whole they differ from us in these respects.

—What is important in your dialogue with the central government? How would you like to see the relationship between state and central government changed?

—It is not an issue of central versus state government. The term "state" is used in different ways. The state, in its scientific sense, is a collection of the political organs of a certain class or of certain classes. Thus, the state is a combination of the central government and the political state. We cannot say that just because we have formal control of the machinery of state in Kerala that we have control over the state machine, because, in the end, the state machinery is in essence the military—it is not on our side. Imagine, for example, that the whole parliamentary system in the state and Delhi were to be abolished. Where would we be then? Where would our power be? Our only power is the formal power we get from bourgeois democracy and its elections. The instant the system dissolves, we will no longer exist. On the other hand, if it remains in force thanks to the military, then Indira Gandhi won't be there either. She can easily be overthrown. It happened in Pakistan. The military is the essential state power. Looked at scientifically, we don't have that power.

—What goals can the Marxist party in Kerala, which has achieved only parliamentary power, set for itself?

—We can use all the power we have to strengthen the revolutionary democratic movement in the whole country.

—What is causing the increasing antagonisms in Indian society—antagonisms between religions, languages, regions, castes, etc?

—To understand them we must examine the social system that has existed in India for a good many centuries. It is based on a combination of what is called the caste system, the village society, and the familial system. These three concepts constitute the totality of Indian society. The caste hierarchy, the family hierarchy—old age and youth on one side, men and women on the other—and the village economy based on natural production, this was the base on which Indian society was built. The caste system is an essential part. Because of the constant mixing of groups and societies from outside and because of the interplay of various religions and philosophies, religious institutions were adopted by the castes; castes, religious orders and tribes all became part of Indian social life. Modernization, capitalist development, the influx of modern education, and bourgeois parliamentary democracy became, on one hand, a tool with which to change the social order; on the other hand, they also reflected this social order in their political institutions.

The fact is that the caste system is losing influence. It isn't as strong as it was when I was a boy. Then, no one in my family would have imagined that I would become an active politician. The system has received strong shocks, but it hasn't been eliminated entirely. Even when it comes to the way the parliamentary system works, in elections, the selection of candidates and the campaign, caste factors still have an influence. That is why caste is said to be a political factor in Kerala—it is partly true. But it is also true that more and more people take part in politics without caste being significant. This breakdown of the old system is happening through an interaction between the new economy and politics, castes, rural societies, village systems and families.

—Can the increase in communalism lead to fascism?

—I wouldn't say that communalism is increasing. Instead I would say that secularization is increasing. It may seem that communalism is increasing because all these caste and religious factors are used by the bourgeois politicians in fighting other factions, but in fact people are uniting. Would anyone have believed, for example, that Hindus and Sikh communalists would unite? But they have; they have built a coalition government. Caste and religion are not the important factors; the important factor is that the bourgeois political system is bankrupt. It shows the growth of factionalism—the genesis of various bourgeois factions attempting to benefit by the split.

—So organizations like RSS are only factions of a dissolving bourgeoisie?

—Yes.

—What is your view of the events in Naxalbari?

—There is a lot of confusion about this issue. The Naxalbari movement itself was a peasant movement for the redistribution of land and the attainment of more rights for the tribal peasants in that area. The peasant masses there wanted to fight for and secure their demands, but some of their top leaders tried to add a political interpretation which said that what was happening in Naxalbari was a politically motivated movement attempting to overthrow the entire political system. They misjudged the mood of the people; but we in the CPI (M) understood what it was. We didn't think, like certain others in the state government, that this was an extremist movement that would fight the police. We said that the demands of the peasants must be met. But we disagreed with those who said this was the beginning of the Indian revolution. We said it had nothing to do with revolution. We said we must examine as many opportunities as possible to strengthen the movement and that this was an opportunity to do so. This is the background of the Naxalbari movement itself. After the movement had started, a number of groups around the country said that it was a real revolution and that we were traitors. But we have told the people that it was not a practical way.

In West Bengal, where there have just been elections, they have carried on a campaign to boycott the elections. The question we asked the voters was: Imagine that we follow the Naxalites' advice and boycott the elections, who will gain by it? Clearly, Atulya Gosh and company.*

* A leader of the Congress (O) party, formerly Secretary of the Congress Committee of West Bengal.—ED.

The so-called Naxalites are small, very noisy groups that the bourgeois press publicizes. The fact is, they are very weak, since their politics doesn't reach the people; people are much more realistic. But we don't condemn the Naxalites as others condemn them. We know that they, with their extremist slogans, are in a way giving expression to the people's dissatisfaction, to the people's disappointment. We are trying to channel all this in a revolutionary way.

—Is there any one reason why small groups such as these have grown all over India?

—Yes, because of a genuine dissatisfaction among the petty bourgeosie, who are both dissatisfied and incapable of organized action. Lenin characterized the petty bourgeois revolutionary as one who is disillusioned with the old generation of bourgeois leaders but isn't capable of organizing as a worker organizes.

—How would you characterize agricultural policy in India since independence?

—The government policy has been one of gradual transformation of the old feudal tenant system to a modern capitalistic system without basically changing it or disturbing the privileges of the old feudal landowners. They don't leave the old feudal landowners untouched but rather reform the feudal landowners into capitalist farmers or capitalist landowners.

—It has been said that if capitalist agriculture just means that the proportion of wage laborers to farmers is increasing, then the amount of capitalist agriculture in India is really increasing. But it has also been said that this is all that is happening and that there isn't any real change in agricultural methods—like increased use of machines—and that there isn't any reduction in precapitalist exploitation forms and the activities of merchants and moneylenders.

—No, I would not say that capitalist agriculture is just

wage labor. Wage labor in itself can mean a modernized version of feudal labor. But that isn't all. It is not correct to say that the use of machines is not growing; techniques really are being improved, though it is clear that methods are not improving on all farms, only in a small sector dominated by capitalistic farmers. A monetization of the agricultural economy is occurring; the use of machinery, fertilizers—all this is increasing. The opportunities for large farms are also increasing.

—Will this result in an upswing in agricultural production?
—No, I believe we are facing a serious crisis in agriculture.

The more and more vocal demands of the state on the central government are a sign of the increased significance of state politics. They may also be a sign of a tendency toward the dissolution of India as a unified state. The unifying struggle against the English is only a memory. The once all-powerful Congress party has split and Indira Gandhi has not managed to gather as many votes as the party got during Nehru's time. The political center of gravity is shifting to the periphery.

Many of the most important Indian politicians choose to run for state parliaments rather than for national office—a sign that the rewards of the former are greater.

The economic center of gravity is shifting to landowners who can exploit the new agricultural methods and "miracle" rices. They have traditionally had very great influence in state politics.

But Kerala also stands for something other than this conflict and for something other than an Indian communism in a position of power. In many ways, Kerala, with its distinctive character, is "India's India"—a rich area with many who are poor and few who are wealthy; where only a small portion of the resources of land and labor can be used; where only a few succeed and many leave; where the majority have so little power over their own lives.

In many respects, the story of Kerala and India is the story of India and the wealthy world.

Naxalbari: the beginning of the revolution?

During the first half of 1967 there was a small peasant revolt in Naxalbari, in northern West Bengal in the narrow tongue of land that connects Assam with the rest of India and divides Nepal from East Pakistan. The peasants in Naxalbari attempted to set up a liberated zone in order to carry through land reform and set up their own political power. They defended this zone against the police of the landowners and government. The peasants were eventually defeated— many were killed or imprisoned.

During the sixties, the landowners had gradually taken over more and more of the land in the area. The landowners also refused to distribute the land, as they were required to do by West Bengal's land reform laws. Most of the land in the area is used by sharecroppers and farmworkers, but there are also large tea plantations in the vicinity.

In March 1967 the peasant dissatisfaction took more active expression. The poor began to appropriate the crops from fields which rightfully ought to have been distributed after the land reform. They plowed up the land which the landowners forced them to leave. In the beginning of March, the landlords fought back, attacked the peasants, and, with the help of police, took back the crops. The peasants, many of whom belonged to the tribal population, and the workers on the tea plantations took up arms (primarily bows and arrows). In May, the communist-led state government, which had come to power in March of the same year, sent a government commission to the area to intervene. The commission was unsuccessful. In June the police put down the rebellion, at least for the time being. The Communist parties denounced the rebellion and expelled members who had taken part. The area affected by the revolt—Naxalbari, Kharibari and Thansidawa—has between one hundred and one hundred fifty thousand inhabitants.

The state government fell later in 1967.

The Naxalbari movement was followed by similar actions throughout India, and the ideas of its leaders, as they are expressed in articles by Kanu Sanyal and Charu Mazumdar in the movement newspapers *Deshabrati* and *Liberation*, have great influence on many in the Indian left. Kanu Sanyal was perhaps the main leader of the Naxalbari revolt and Charu Mazumdar its theoretician.

The Naxalbari movement is a peasant movement. Its adherents consider the liberation of the other oppressed classes possible only if the peasants are liberated—80 percent of India's population lives in the villages. "Naxalites" describe India as a half-feudal, half-colonial country where the main conflict is between the people and the feudal lords. Therefore, the peasants constitute the main force in the anti-imperialist and antifeudal fight. The state apparatus maintains the feudal system by violent means and the only way to crush this armed rule is by armed revolt.

The struggle in Naxalbari was not primarily cver land, according to the Naxalites; land was only a minor issue: the main issue was political power, state power. This power can be gained only through armed struggle in revolution—in Naxalbari, through guerrilla war. According to the Naxalbari movement, this is a fundamental difference between them and the bourgeois and petty bourgeois parties, including India's two Communist parties. We cannot, they say, attach the antifeudal struggle to the issue of land distribution and look at this issue as a question of social justice alone. We must instead crush oppression by breaking down the political, economic, social, and cultural structure which maintains feudal exploitation. This can be done only if the peasants themselves establish a new political power in the villages—the power of revolutionary peasant committees. The peasants must rise and arm themselves, organize guerrilla groups, create liberated areas, and gradually build a people's army. A fight for land alone is nothing more than isolationism; the agrarian revolution, according to the Naxalites, is something much greater than insuring social justice for the peasants.

In order to gain political, economic, and military power, the Naxalites began to set up revolutionary peasant committees in the villages in Naxalbari in March and April of 1967. The peasants armed themselves and divided the land. According to Kanu Sanyal in an article in *Liberation*, 90 percent of the peasants in the area were organized in this way (70 percent of the peasants in the area were poor and landless, 20 percent are middle peasants, and 10 percent are wealthy peasants). Sanyal notes the following accomplishments of the revolt:

1. All land now owned and used by the peasants themselves was divided by the peasant committees. Thus the old political, economic, and social structure in the villages, based on monopolistic landholding, was broken.

2. All land registers and other documents having to do with land had been used to trick the peasants; therefore, all such documents were burned.

3. All agreements between peasants and *jotedar*s (large landholders) and between peasants and moneylenders were declared invalid. They had been entered into under inequitable conditions and often represented gross injustices to the peasants.

4. The *jotedar*s had hidden large quantities of rice in order to create an artificial food shortage that would push up prices. This rice and other possessions which belonged to the *jotedar*s were taken over by the peasants and distributed among them.

5. Those *jotedar*s who were long known as especially harsh oppressors and those who opposed the peasant struggle were condemned to death by the peasants.

6. Those known as collaborators with the oppressors and the police were tried openly. Some were condemned to death, others were paraded through the village under humiliating circumstances.

7. In order to defend themselves against the expected attack from the state, the peasants armed themselves with their traditional weapons, spears and bows, and with weapons they had managed to take from the *jotedar*s.

8. The internal administration of the villages, a sentry system, and regular school attendance were organized.

9. The political power of the peasants in the area was exercised through regional and central revolutionary committees.

10. The old laws which had served only the previous rulers were replaced by measures of the revolutionary committees.

According to Kanu Sanyal, the leadership of the struggle was in the hands of the landless, who were the most militant and were against any form of compromise with feudalism. In the beginning, the middle peasants were suspicious and remained aloof; they joined when they saw that the struggle was directed against the *jotedars*, the landowners, and the moneylenders, and that it was in their interest to support it. This meant a great deal for the scope of the struggle. In the beginning, the wealthy farmers were totally against the fight, being often exploiters themselves and therefore afraid of the consequences. They tried in every way to criticize the rebellious peasants and acted as spies in the *jotedars*' behalf. But when the middle peasants began to support the side of the poor peasants, the rich farmers stopped opposing the movement and remained neutral from then on. The other important group in Naxalbari, the tea plantation workers, wholeheartedly supported the peasant struggle. They struck, armed themselves, and closed ranks behind the peasants.

Kanu Sanyal feels that the revolutionary situation in India at present is excellent. American imperialism is in an acute crisis; the conflicts between the imperialists are becoming more bitter and the conflicts between domestic and foreign capital are increasing. The economic plans of the ruling Congress party are falling apart; the people are suffering more and more from India's harsh economic crisis, and their confidence in the previously dominant Congress party has received a serious blow—as was demonstrated by the defeat of the Congress party in the latest election.

Why did the peasant revolt fail—if only temporarily—in Naxalbari? What mistakes do the Naxalbari leaders themselves think they made?

In the first place, they feel that they lacked a strong party organization "armed with Marxist-Leninist theory and its highest development in the current era, Mao Tse-tung's thought" and closely tied to the mass of the people. What party organization there was was led by the petty-bourgeois elements which remained passive the entire time. "The

205

peasant movements have been dependent on party leaders belonging to the intelligentsia. Consequently, they begin their movements with speeches by leaders and the organization of peasant divisions through open propaganda campaigns. Such movements are, of course, completely dependent on their top leaders and therefore run out of steam whenever these leaders from the intelligentsia decide to stop them. Since all the agitation and the whole movement is out in the open, the whole organization is defenseless when confronted by repressive measures. . . . The revolutionary intellectuals must work underground from the very start. Only then will they be forced to be dependent on the peasant revolutionaries." So explains Charu Mazumdar.

The struggle could not be developed because a broad base was never built and because there was not enough faith in the people. "We now openly admit that we did not have faith in the heroic peasant masses, which, quickly as a storm, constructed revolutionary peasant committees, accomplished the ten goals and quickly extended the class struggle during the period of April–September 1967" (Kanu Sanyal). The leaders were afraid of going too far, of forcing their will upon the peasants from above.

Too little weight was placed on the military aspect; the enemy's strength was underestimated in the first stage of the struggle. Since communists dominated the West Bengal government, it was not believed that they would hit the peasant uprising so hard. Later, when the people were prepared to fight back against the enemy, the enemy's strength was overestimated and the consequences exaggerated. The result was that the people became confused and lacked leadership when the government began to terrorize the peasants. The populace was armed, but never created an organized armed force. In the liberated areas, there were no guerrilla forces for defense.

So much for the leaders of the Naxalbari movement. The first rebellion was put down by the state regime. At the end of May 1967, hundreds of peasants were imprisoned and some were killed in the fighting. Since then the persecution has continued and most of the movement's leaders have been killed or put in prison. In 1969-70, new fighting broke out.

In Naxalbari, the "second level of the struggle" is now taking place—the level of construction. Revolutionary bases in the countryside are being built up; many intellectuals and students have left the cities and joined the peasants. The peasant revolt in Naxalbari has had a deep effect on political life throughout India. In the Terai area at the foot of the Himalayas, poor peasants have armed themselves and occupied uncultivated government-owned land. Fighting has broken out and a number of peasants have been killed by police. In southern Bihar, Andhra Pradesh, Orissa, and Tamil Nadu, similar rebellions are going on and thousands upon thousands of poor peasants are revolting against oppression. In most states there are at least some areas where similar peasant revolts have occurred during the last few years.

According to fairly unanimous information from both the Communist parties and the "Naxalites," the peasant revolts are flaring up *outside* the Communist parties. In most cases, the Communist parties are strongly opposed to these groups, the so-called leftist Communists—the Communist Party of India (Marxist)—more so than the rightist Communists—the Communist Party of India—since they have lost more members to the "Naxalites." Communist reaction to this radicalization of the peasants has been mixed. They try to make the "Naxalites" suspect, either by calling them CIA agents who are trying to split the communist movement even more than it is already, or by calling them Chinese agents (China has had a very poor reputation since the border war of 1962); but they have also tried to capture this radicalism with their own, slightly "milder," programs—programs aimed at occupation of uncultivated land, but with political power won at the ballot box.

Asked how he felt about the attempts at armed revolution now going on in Latin America, CPI Chairman S. A. Dange replied:

"They are good. Conditions are so bad that people can't wait any longer." How are conditions in India then, he was asked. Can people here wait for elections every fifty years? "Yes, they can."

In the meantime, the scattered "Naxalites" are organizing themselves on a national basis. In October 1968, groups from various parts of the country met for the first time and created the "Coordinating Committee of Communist Revolutionaries," but even this movement does not seem to be free from the antagonisms which have divided every communist movement in India for so long. Personal and regional antagonisms make cooperation difficult.

India is a big country where a great deal can happen without jeopardizing the stability of the whole. A war can be going on in one part of the country without people knowing about it in another part. A peasant revolt can be going on in one part of a state without affecting the peasants in another part of the same state. It is not certain that the radicalization of the peasants now going on in certain parts of India is numerically the most important tendency in the countryside. Perhaps, for example, the number of peasants turning fascist is greater than the number taking up arms in the spirit of the Naxalbari movement. India is a country with a well-developed communications network and a relatively effective and strong defense force—a defense force which could, thus far, count on support both from the United States and Russia; a defense force which can be used inside as well as outside India. India's administration is, all things considered, not a Kuomintang-style administration. And the larger part of the country is densely populated plainsland without cover vegetation and therefore unsuitable for guerrilla warfare of the conventional type.

Perhaps Naxalbari does not stand for the Indian revolution, but Naxalbari introduced a series of peasant revolts, a movement which gives the impression not of being stagnant but rather of accelerating. For many peasants, Naxalbari has meant political consciousness. Political stability in India—a stability in the service of the privileged—may tolerate several Naxalbaris, but what will happen if peasants create liberated zones in ten places? If a radicalized communist movement grows under the influence of these peasant movements, choosing to work outside Parliament's paralyzing atmosphere? How will the frustrated middle class react? A military coup is possible but it would have serious consequences for national solidarity—the armed forces are almost entirely recruited from certain groups of people in northern India and a military coup would further complicate the antagonisms between northern and southern India.

Perhaps Naxalbari does stand for the Indian revolution.

seven party leaders' views about Naxalbari

S. A. Dange, leader of the Communist party of India. The CPI is the so-called rightist Communist party; it received 5 percent of the vote in the 1971 election.

"The Naxalbari incident was a revolt of a farming

REVOLUTION

A common belief in the West is that Indians are sunk in a religious apathy in which they have always quietly accepted suffering. This is false.

There are many examples of revolt and rebellion in India's history. Revolts and revolutionary movements are now happening in many places. Even the very poorest, the farmworkers and the oppressed tribesmen, are now beginning to organize themselves and fight—with violent means if necessary—to improve their condition.

The caste system, by its division of people into well-defined groups with strong internal loyalties, has obstructed solidarity across caste boundaries.

But in some of the protest movements that are now growing, a new kind of solidarity can be seen—a solidarity that reaches outside the traditional groups, where the oppressed join forces, regardless of caste, religion or language.

When destitute farmworkers—the poorest of the poor, those oppressed even by the oppressed—now close ranks to take the crops and land from the landowners to divide among themselves, it is an extremely important development. Revolts in India have always been begun mainly by those who have already come up a little way from the bottom; only recently have the very poorest been involved.

Only when these hundreds of millions of poor people take their future in their own hands will India's poverty and oppression be brought to an end.

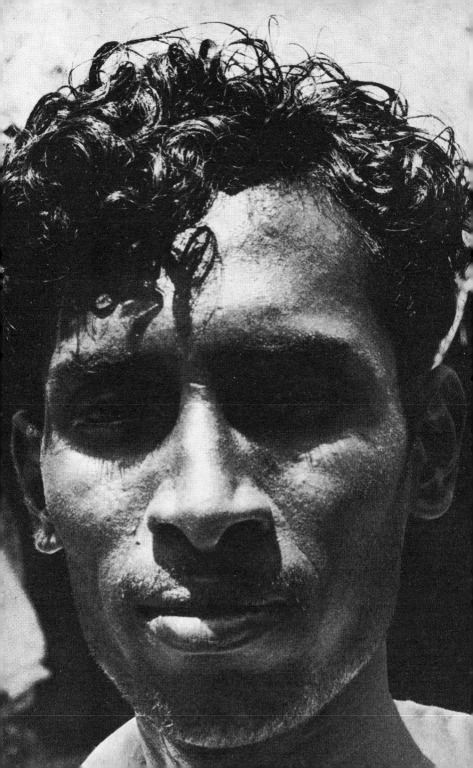

tribal population which was very oppressed by the land-owning pattern in the area. Because they were led by a group of people who called themselves communists who followed Mao Tse-tung's thoughts, the matter received greater publicity than it deserved. It was treated as a peasant revolt. Since it was believed by certain people in the area to be an experiment in Mao Tse-tung's thought, it has now gotten an international name, and a special school of thought in India among certain communist groups is now called Naxalbari communism. But it was really a peasant revolt. It was not an armed revolt, because the peasants had only bows and arrows while the landowners had rifles, and it was soon cleared up by the police. Nor did it flare up for any other reason. In West Bengal at the time there was an elected leftist democratic government. The government tried to meet the peasants' main demands and to protect them. The name remains because of its political significance, not because of its economic significance."

S. M. Joshi, leader, at the time of the interview, of the Samyukta Socialist party, an ultranationalist social democratic party which received 2 percent of the vote in the latest election, mostly in Bihar and Uttar Pradesh.

"Naxalbari is very strategically oriented because it is on our border. Some people believe, despite the fact they call themselves Marxists, that they were completely logical when they tried to make a revolution by fighting with the landowners there; but they forget the fact that India is a gigantic country, and that they couldn't succeed if they tried to do it at that place. Another thing was that they were too dependent upon outsiders. The *Peking Review* applauded them the whole time. I visited the area myself; I wrote an article about it for the *Times of India* in which I said, 'I have nothing against your struggle if it is peaceful and without violence. I would not have anything against that. Your party is now leading the government. If you do this it means that you aren't following the rules of the game. If you have the power in your hands you ought to legislate. You have the majority, you can give the land to these people. Why are you making this fuss? If you do it peacefully, I have nothing against it. But if you take to weapons, I am opposed.' "

A. B. Vajpayee, leader of Jan Sangh, the second largest opposition party. Jan Sangh received 7 percent of the vote in the last election and has strength almost solely in northern India, where it has gained great popularity during recent years—primarily among the middle classes in the cities—with its right-wing extremist, Hindu-fanatic politics.

"Naxalbari opened the eyes of those who believed that the communists had begun using democratic means to achieve their goals. Naxalbari was a great warning that it is difficult for the communists to change. They had their government in West Bengal; they could have reduced the limit on how much land one may own if they had really wanted to help the landless farmworkers. They could have done it with the machinery of government. But in Naxalbari they wanted to take the law into their own hands and everything they did was to strengthen the party, not to help the landless. I visited Naxalbari and the peasants complained to me that the communists took their crops and sold them at the market, but the money was not dealt out among the landless. They put the money in the party fund. Those who didn't support the communists suffered, whether they were rich or poor. Poor peasants were persecuted too, in some cases murdered or robbed, because they hadn't supported the Communist party. Naxalbari was an attempt to terrorize the peasants so they would place themselves under the dictatorship of the Communist party, but the attempt failed."

P. Ramamurthi, leader of the parliamentary group of the Communist Party of India (Marxist). CPI (M) is often called the leftist Communists, but the differences *within* both the large Communist parties are greater than the differences between them. The CPI(M) received 6 percent of the vote in the 1971 elections.

"There are not many people who know what happened in Naxalbari. In Naxalbari there is a tribal population problem. There were a number of people in the tribal populace whose land had been taken from them. The government legislated against this situation, but the laws were never enforced. If the Naxalbari movement had concerned itself with occupying land and thereby forced the government to solve their problem, it would have been good; there would not have been difficulty. But the issue of occupation never came up because the land is not farmed at that time of year, in May. They just went and put up red flags in a number of fields. If it had stopped there, it would not have been any problem. But then some robberies and other things occurred, so we sent our minister and he talked with the people. He said, 'Keep your land even if it is owned by the large landowners, but don't take land from the small farmers. You'll have to fight the large landholders if you make everyone your enemy—then you'll be through.' And he said that they shouldn't give up: 'You can give in on certain small issues, but not when it concerns the main issues.' They accepted this, but later they changed their minds and said, 'We are not fighting for land, we are fighting for the power here.' And then the problem came up. The question of fighting to gain power is not part of this issue; you cannot take power with bows and arrows. It is there that our opinions differ. We said that we could not fight in this way. In the Indian situation, power can only be gained by combining the struggle of the working class and the peasants. This country is not Vietnam or China; this country is a land with a highly developed communications system, and a centralized police and military administration. How can we overcome this special problem? If we go the same way as the Naxalbari movement, we will just fall into the hands of the central government's police. That won't get us anywhere. We agree completely on mobilizing the peasants to occupy the land, but when they talk about establishing their own state power under these conditions, then we say that it just gives our opponents the chance to use terrible repression, which the Naxalbari movement has no chance of surviving."

N. G. Ranga, leader of Swatantra, which received 3 percent of the vote in the last election. Swatantra gets most of its support from the rural landowning class; its facade has not prevented it from exploiting communalistic tensions in Indian society. The party's communalism has increased since Ranga came to power.

"Naxalbari was a communistic experiment. It is true that there was oppression of the landless, and even more of the sharecroppers. There was need of legislation to protect these people. They had long been ignored by the Congress administration there. The Communists succeeded in taking advantage of this fact and started to cause trouble. But it wasn't nearly as bad as the Communists portrayed it, and could easily have been solved if a regime oriented toward the problems of the peasants had been in power."

Surendra Mohan, joint secretary of the Praja Socialist party, a social democratic party in search of an image which received only 1 percent of the vote in the last election.

"What happened in Naxalbari was very unfortunate. In the first place, Naxalbari is located, geographically and strategically, at a point where India, Nepal and East Pakistan meet; just nine miles divide Nepal and Pakistan, and China is not so far away. So the kind of movement that took place in Naxalbari would have had serious consequences if it had cut the connection between Assam and the rest of India. If it was necessary to start a movement for the distribution of land, it should have been started in areas where there isn't this larger scale, as in Midnapur and Burdhwan. Ultimately, that's what I don't understand! When the Naxalbari movement took place, there was a coalition regime in West Bengal, led mainly by Communists, especially leftist Communists—the same element that started the movement in Naxalbari. The best way to solve the landowning problems in West Bengal would have been for the coalition regime to have immediately passed laws against the injustices; instead, the leftist Communists tried to agitate, which, in a way, meant agitating against their own government. We couldn't understand all this, and we think that it was part of a plan intended to create strategic difficulties for India and to cut off a large portion of northeastern India from the rest of the country."

Siddavanahalli Nijalingappa, at the time leader of the Congress party, undisputedly the largest party and the only party which has headed the Union government since independence. The Congress party received 41 percent of the vote in the 1967 election. During the fall of 1969, the party split into two factions—the ruling Congress party, under the leadership of Indira Gandhi, with 43 percent of the vote in the 1971 election, and the new rightist party, Congress (O), led by Nijalingappa, which received 10 percent of the vote and so became the largest opposition party:

"Naxalbari was a very sad story. I don't think it ought to be repeated ... We cannot tolerate another Naxalbari. It was antidemocratic, antisocial, and ugly. I wouldn't want it to happen anyplace else and I would fight it. I deeply disapprove of it. We don't want such a thing to happen again."

the tribespeople: the oppressed in revolt

Anigara

Anigara is located deep in the jungle in southern Bihar. We go a long way on foot, led by the district government supervisor, to reach the village, which is almost hidden in the vegetation. Anigara is one of the villages of the *Munda* people, one of India's tribes. A million Indians belong to the Munda. Every twelfth Indian—approximately forty million people—belongs to the tribal population, perhaps the country's most oppressed minority. They are economically exploited, socially disadvantaged, and despised even by the casteless.

The origin of the tribesmen is uncertain, but many consider them to be India's original inhabitants. For thousands of years, they were driven into the mountains and the forests, first by the Dravidians and then by the so-called Aryans.

Anigara. Mud huts; people and animals; tiny rice fields; wells; a path that leads right through the village. The first thing we see—the school, a sign that Anigara is a privileged village. The school building is a whitewashed earthen shed with a dirt floor, wooden benches, and a blackboard. The teachers show us around; we sit at a table in the schoolyard and they ask us how much a Swedish teacher earns. The government civil servant translates somewhat reluctantly. The injustices are written in the air between us; in their eyes and raised eyebrows. Some try to seem unmoved; yes of course, yes, Sweden. Others act surprised. We drink tea with ginger and talk a little about the school before we wander around the village. It is harvest time. Dusk is falling over the fields; the people have gone home after the day's work. It is very beautiful; a yellow light rests over the landscape; soft mountains at the horizon. We are looked at curiously, but we are not the first foreigners here. Anigara sometimes has visitors from far away, but until now only anthropologists.

It quickly becomes dark and we follow the path back to the schoolyard where a storm lantern spreads its bright light. Here we sit drinking rice wine in plastic mugs with the village schoolteacher and the supervisor-interpreter and the sound of drums. The villagers will dance and sing for us and talk about everything that previous guests have been interested in: their festivals, their taboos, the totems they worship, how a man buys a bride, how old they are when they get to sleep with one another.

The village inhabitants gather around us. The men stand separate, with straight backs, very serious at first. Some have threadbare woolen shawls on their shoulders, but most are bare from the waist up. The women and children stand a bit farther away, a little more giggly. The interpreter acts like a friend. He places the schoolteacher, a Munda from Anigara, beside himself. He tells us:

"The tribe is divided into a number of clans. One may not marry within his own clan but still must marry within the tribe. A Munda must marry another Munda. It is considered a sin to have sexual relations with someone in the same clan. If it happens the punishment is severe; the sinner is expelled from the village and the society.

"Each clan is bound to some kind of totem. This totem object is holy for the clan. It is believed that this object is related to the forefathers in some way. For example, the totem object can be a certain kind of root; the clan which has this root for a totem is forbidden to eat it, since it is believed that they are descended from it.

"When a marriage is to be arranged it is not considered good for the bridegroom to take part in the preparations. It is also unwise for him to know the bride before he marries her, but this doesn't mean that there are any restrictions on boys and girls before they marry. They are allowed to be together however they wish. It is only after marriage that the restrictions come in. A married woman may not have any sexual relations outside marriage.

"The marriage preparations begin with the boy's father arranging for an intermediary to go to the intended bride's home and make arrangements. The price of the bride is decided—the common price is two oxen, twelve rupees, and five or six pieces of cloth. The boy and girl must also agree to the marriage. The village elder then advises the girl to offer the boy a bowl of water to drink. If one of them doesn't fulfill his or her part of the ceremony there is no marriage. This is not just an empty ritual; it often happens that one of them says no, most often the boy. When the boy's father is on his way to the girl's house, it is very significant if he sees lucky or unlucky signs on the way. If he meets a snake, for example, it is lucky, but if he sees a crow cawing or an old woman with an empty bowl or someone chopping wood, it is unlucky, and the wedding cannot take place as planned."

We try, despite the interpreter's apparent unwillingness, to switch the conversation over to their economic circumstances and what they themselves think about their living conditions. We ask how the land is distributed.

"There is almost only poor land here, the kind of land that rice cannot be cultivated on. Most of the families in the village have about two or three acres of land each. The land is poor and one family consists of between five and eight people, so such a little piece of land doesn't provide enough food for more than two months. The rest of the year we must live on roots, fruits and leaves. If we can, we try to get work on the side. Some go to the north to look for work on the tea plantations in Assam or to get a job in Calcutta. We do whatever we can to find work.

"There are four or five families in the village who have more than thirty acres, but twenty families have nothing at all. Twenty families of the village's seventy. They must take whatever work they can get—day laborers in agriculture, servants in a family, perhaps something in the city. The wages run around one and a half rupees per day. Women get one rupee."

"What are the biggest changes here in the village during the last five to ten years?" Our question is followed by a long silence. Finally someone answers.

"An electric line has been brought into the village. And now there is a school in the village too, but there are no newspapers, books, or radio programs in our language. Economically, everything is like before."

"What needs changing most of all?"

"Most important of all is that we get more land."

"How?"

"There is land that no one cultivates. We want permission to cultivate it. But it isn't just that so few families own more than thirty acres when twenty families don't have any at all. Everyone should have the same. The government ought to see that everyone gets the same."

We ask how many of the village's children go to school. The interpreter answers quickly: "All of them." We try again, asking the village people this time, with the help of a school-teacher who knows a little English. "How many children of school age are there here?"

"Approximately seventy."

"How many of them go to school?"

"Thirty."

"How many girls are there here and how many of them go to school?"

"Of thirty-five girls, only seven go to school."

People around us have now begun to talk; they eagerly answer, interrupting each other. The interpreter glares at us at every question. Since some of the teachers know a little English, he must translate everything faithfully. Finally, he suggests that the dancing and music begin. "These kinds of political questions have never been asked before," he mutters. On the way home, he confides in us his opinion that it was much better under the English. "If you meet any of the government bigshots in Delhi, ask them why in the hell they created my job," he says as we leave Anigara in the pitch-black night, watching for snakes on the road.

The Economy

India's tribesmen are usually described as primitive people who live in isolation, without cultural or economic contact with the outside world. This isolation is usually given as the reason for their poverty. But the traditional picture excludes much of the reality that affects the tribal population. The tribes are hardly isolated, either culturally or economically.

The *Adivasi*s, as the tribes are called in India, have been involved in a constant interchange with the surrounding

Hindu culture. Many of the castes lowest on the social ladder are really tribes. Many Hindu customs and ideas come from tribal religions. The tribespeople have most often been disadvantaged and have, for example, a much lower literacy rate than the average for India. At the last census, the literacy rate for the whole country was given as 24 percent but for the Adivasis it was only 8 percent.

Traditionally, the tribal economy is based entirely on what the land and the forest can provide. India is a big country and there has always been a great deal of land and forest, but wherever India's population grew, the tribes were driven away. They had to be satisfied with the worst land in the mountains and whatever was left of the rugged jungle—anything that no one else wanted to cultivate. When the English let moneylenders and merchants into the reservations during the eighteenth and nineteenth centuries, the tribal population went into debt and in many cases had to leave their land. The English took over the forests.

Since independence there have been several attempts at land reform which would give the land back to the Adivasis, but they were so unsuccessful that it had to be officially admitted that nothing was changed. The Adivasis are still dependent on what the land and forest can provide—90 percent of them are employed in forestry or agriculture (the figure is 70 percent for the entire Indian population).

The condition of the tribespeople has not improved during recent years. They seldom own the land they use; it is owned by moneylenders and landowners who do not belong to the tribes. What land the Adivasis have managed to keep is the worst—too poor even for rice cultivation. They can sell the produce only through merchants who don't belong to the tribes. The merchants buy the crops at low prices and later sell them at high prices when there is a lack of food; they are often aligned with the moneylenders, who exploit the

Adivasis' distress and illiteracy. Interest rates are so high that it is nearly impossible for anyone who has once borrowed ever to be free of debt. Once a man has parted with his land and possessions, he has nothing to sell but his labor. In this way many Adivasis become bound for life to work for the same person, often under unbearable conditions.

The Adivasi is thus incorporated into an economic system stretching far outside the tribe, an economic system in which he is the weak, exploited part. He is exploited as a landless worker by the landowner who comes from "outside." If he produces anything he can sell it only through a merchant from "outside" who pays him low prices and sells at great profit. If he produces some slight surplus over and above what he absolutely needs for himself, it often goes to the moneylender in payment of a loan. The moneylender is not an Adivasi and he does not invest his money in anything productive among the Adivasis.

Such is the overall economic situation of India's many Adivasis. There are exceptions, of course; here and there one finds Adivasi landowners, moneylenders belonging to the tribe, etc. There are also a few tribes which have succeeded in raising themselves out of the misery they were forced into.

The Adivasis have not been patiently resigned to poverty. More than any other group of people in India, time and again they have revolted against the landowners and moneylenders. In today's troubed and unstable India, it is among the tribal population that the most frequent and most violent revolts have flared up.

Rebellion among the Girijans

An example of tribal unrest is the Girijan tribe, which lives in Srikakulam in central India. The eighty thousand Girijans constitute more than 90 percent of the population of this area. Despite this, there are only a few Girijans among all the landowners, moneylenders and merchants in the area.

There are two types of villages in the area, plains villages and mountain villages. Those not belonging to the tribal populace live only in the plains villages, which are central for trade in the area. The poor Girijans must come to them if they wish to sell or buy anything.

Only Girijans live in the small villages on the mountain slopes. The merchants have gradually been taking over the Girijans' land by selling them necessities like kerosene, salt, and tobacco on credit.

By the end of the 1950s the Girijans had lost nearly all their fertile land. They had become day laborers, underpaid and oppressed. The common daily wage was pushed down to less than ten cents. Those who managed to get part of their old land on lease had to pay up to two-thirds of the crop to the new landowners. The need to procure necessities on credit increased. The consequence has been that nowadays a son does not inherit his father's wealth but rather his debts.

In the early 1960s, the Girijans began to demand that the land be given back to its former owners. They began, quite simply, to confiscate the landowners' crops. Young men replaced the tribe's traditional leaders—young men who had been educated in the city and then returned to their villages, where they had managed to formulate the tribe's dissatisfaction and to pursue the ideas of justice and equality better than the traditional leaders.

The revolt increased in scope and intensity. With mass meetings and strikes, the Girijans tried to force the landowners to raise wages. They agitated heavily in the villages.

The merchants were forced to sell their goods for fair prices, and, because of the inner solidarity of the village, the moneylenders were prevented from demanding payments.

Small village schools were started and adult education was begun.

Between the early sixties and the middle of 1967, the Girijans got many of their demands. Wages were raised, rents cut in half, close to seventeen hundred acres of land were retaken, and four thousand acres of wasteland were cultivated—something not previously permitted. Loans amounting to three hundred thousand rupees were written off, and prices became more just. In the summer of 1967, however, the picture changed. By that time, peasant revolts had flared up in many places in India and the government now took stern measures to nip the Girijans' revolution in the bud.

Several clashes had previously taken place with landowners and their men in cooperation with the local police, but when seven platoons of specially armed police were stationed in the area, the scale of the fighting increased. During the early part of 1968, they raided 226 mountain villages and arrested fifteen hundred Girijans. Four Girijans were killed during the fighting.

The clashes intensified during 1969 as a consequence of the police activity. Political activity among the Girijans became more militant and was driven underground. The fighting is now more extensive—groups of a thousand or more Girijans attack landowners, who receive aid from the armed police.

The poor farmworkers have begun to take over more and more land, dividing it among themselves. In an encounter between police and tribesmen at the end of May 1969, twelve Girijans were killed.

The leaders of the revolt speak of Srikakulam as India's Yenan.*

* The communists' base area during the Chinese Revolution.—ED.

the revolutionary

Interview with T. Nagi Reddy

T. Nagi Reddy, revolutionary leader in Andhra Pradesh. We meet him at his home in Hyderabad the day he leaves Parliament, some hours before he is to take the train to his home district and leave this residence of parliamentary leaders for good.

He comes rushing in with his portfolio under his arm and a contented expression on his face. He looks rather young, has a finely chiseled face and intense eyes; he smiles a lot and talks a lot. We are interrupted occasionally during the interview by Indian journalists coming in and asking why he left Parliament. He gave a fiery speech earlier in the day and exhorted the peasants to extraparliamentary methods and armed struggle, so his is the biggest name in India today. His wife is a little bewildered but says that this was not unexpected. Now she must pack up the little they own and follow her husband out into the countryside. She was a very poor girl from a southern village when she met her lifelong companion. She doesn't really understand politics, she sighs, with a glance toward the little bookshelf where Lenin's collected works stand in a row. She is very thin and delicate, has her black hair tied in a knot over the back of her neck, wears glasses, and is dressed in a brown sari. She has devoted her life mostly to raising her daughter who is now married and lives in Delhi. She smiles slightly at her husband when he rushes off for the train with a small suitcase in his hand.

T. Nagi Reddy has the greatest national reputation among revolutionary Indian communist leaders. He was purged from the CPI (M) in 1967 and left his parliamentary post in Andhra Pradesh in 1969. He led the committee which was set up to organize the various revolutionary movements in the country.

—What are the most important problems in India today?

—The farming problem. During the last two or three years the problem has become more and more acute, with the result that numerous revolts are now going on, both organized and unorganized. The oppression by the landowners is growing, but so is the people's resistance. When there is an organization, the people's resistance continues to grow, but when there is no organization, it explodes and dies out. Our duty is to see that this mobilization of the anti-landowner fight gets organized in such a way that it will continue to grow in intensity and will culminate in armed struggle. Without armed struggle, it cannot survive. Without armed struggle, a revolution cannot succeed.

—What will your greatest difficulties be?

—The difficulties are of course our own mistakes during the last sixteen years, which have naturally led us to a condition of disorganization. To be frank, we are not organized in the way we ought to be if we are to function in a revolutionary way. We have created illusions among the people about parliamentary democracy. We have, during these sixteen years of parliamentary action, organized the Communist party's revolutionary machinery in a very parliamentary way. The old discipline has been lost. The old unselfish tendency has gone to waste; the old hard work has disappeared. Everything that a revolutionary needs has been lost. We must rebuild. This will be our greatest difficulty.

—Where is the struggle most developed right now?

—I would say that right now there is no really great struggle going on at all. A few years ago the people in Naxalbari had a revolt. Now a rebellion is going on in Srikakulam. There will be rebellions here and there in the country during the near future. Organizing them all will take time—it will surely take two or three years—but we must work patiently toward this goal and organize the peasants in different places so that they are coordinated during the rest of the struggle. In Andhra we are trying to reorient our organization to concentrate on base areas where we can fight and hold out in our struggle.

—What role will the cities play?

—We will, of course, support every democratic struggle of the middle class or working class, but the cities will play only a secondary role. They will never be able to play a leading role in a revolution, especially not in a country like India. The leaders of the revolution must come from the agricultural areas, because it is in the agricultural areas that the economic crisis is most intense; it is there that the peasants' oppression is greatest. The people can also hold out in their struggle in the agricultural areas longer than they can in the cities.

—What role will be played by the various sectors among the peasants—farmworkers, small peasants, middle peasants?

—In India the situation is such that the dominant feudal landowners take advantage of the capitalist economy. They now have greater political and economic advantages than they had under the English. So what could happen is that the middle peasants and everyone below them could be unified in the struggle against the landowners. This might even include

the smaller landowners. The very biggest landowners sometimes have quarrels with these smaller landowners and the
small landowners would like to see an end to the hegemony
of the large landowners. So the very biggest of the feudal
landowners will be our first target and we will not spread
enmity between ourselves and the small landowners; we want
them on our side as far as possible. Today the feudal landowners are the greatest danger, and our fight will be primarily
against them.

—Will parliamentary action have any meaning in this
struggle to liberate the peasants?

—For the present we don't think so.

—You left the state parliament today.

—Yes, but if we had been carrying on the working-class
struggle in its revolutionary form during these sixteen years,
we could probably have also used Parliament, even if an
agrarian revolution is going on in some places. India is a
gigantic subcontinent; it has many different organizational
and revolutionary requirements.

We can go in for armed struggle in a really large area and
still sit in Parliament in other areas where no armed struggle
is going on. This would probably have been the best way to
organize the revolutionary struggle—sometimes parlia-
mentarily and sometimes extraparliamentarily. Trying now to
organize both is meaningless. As for the future, we must wait
and see how things develop, how successful our organization's work is and how the coordination of all these struggles
goes. Then we must consider very clearly the various tactical
possibilities open to us.

—What are the greatest difficulties in your work of politicizing the peasants—when it comes to their attitudes, for
example?

—When you get right down to it, the peasant has a very
conservative attitude since he is so severely oppressed today

—economically, socially, and politically. But the peasants' conservative attitudes are no hindrance when they begin to fight; that has been our experience. The opportunities I can see today are greater than those of two or three years ago, for example. The peasants are getting disillusioned with the parliamentary line; the peasants are getting disillusioned with this kind of rule; the peasants are getting disillusioned with everything. If we don't intervene they will become demoralized. We must now see to it that they don't become demoralized by all these disappointments, but rather take part in struggle so that they understand that only they themselves can save the situation. No one else can do it, only they themselves.

—What role do the imperialists play in the oppression of Indian peasants?

—Good God! Their role is the most basic role one can imagine. The encroachment of foreign monopoly on the Indian agricultural economy is growing very rapidly, especially now that the Congress regime is attempting to develop what is called capitalist farming in everything new being introduced—fertilizers, pesticides, new seed, cooperation. In some places the monopolies are directly involved in the produce trade. The imperialists encroach upon and take over all these areas. Unfortunately, the revolutionary left did not foresee this, so it has never been explained to the peasant masses in such a way that they could understand it. I am afraid that many within the so-called left in Parliament still do not understand the tremendous significance of this imperialist penetration into the agricultural economy. It is only during the last year that we have begun to study the problem in its correct perspective and have attempted to understand the depth of this penetration. I think that the peasant problem is not just a problem of feudalism, which is an external, visible enemy; there is also a big anti-imperialist problem, concerning prices and markets, concerning the goods they need.

—What were the biggest mistakes of the Naxalbari movement?

—To tell the truth, I have not studied the Naxalbari struggle in detail. Not every armed struggle, whether in Naxalbari or some other place, will be a continuous series of victories. If every armed struggle was an unbroken string of victories, we could say that it was only a question of two or three years; but there will be many successes and many failures. The fact is that Naxalbari stands for a new way of thinking that is now making its mark in many places throughout the country, far out into the isolated villages. In this respect, Naxalbari was a great success; but if we think in terms of armed struggle, its continuation, a continuous series of armed successes—then Naxalbari is no success. But if you expected it to be so, then you were an optimist, not a revolutionary. Naxalbari could not be a success of this sort. Nor is it good to believe that Srikakulam will be a series of successes without small defeats. It's not even like that in Vietnam; how could we expect it of Naxalbari?

—A completely different question. Can the European left play any part in your struggle?

—Oh yes! An enormously important part. But I don't expect material aid. What I expect is that the left will explain to the European people that this struggle is now being carried out by the peasants in the villages. I also expect the left to explain the political and economic background of what is happening, and that the struggle will lead to the final national war of liberation in this country. People will not understand that this is a question of a war of liberation now that India is politically independent. Unfortunately, this has never really been true, even if it seems that we became self-governing. Now it is completely clear that our independence was a false independence. Therefore, you must be able to explain that the agrarian revolution is a result of the political, economic, and social domination of the present imperialist powers. This domination is actually greater now than it was in 1947. I notice it even in my daily life, in a way that I didn't in 1947. The universities were not so flooded by European thought as they are now. When I was a student, I was more independent politically. There was more political thinking, more national thinking than today's Indian students experience. This is due to the encroachment of imperialism on our universities. Such encroachments occur everywhere. You must be able to explain all this to your own people and tell them that among students, the middle class, workers, peasants—everywhere—at some level the struggle against imperialism is being fought.

A note on the interviews

This book contains scarcely a single fact not supported in the interview material or in quoted sources. Interviews with people from various classes, castes, religions, language groups and states not only gave us the basic knowledge of the country and concrete facts; they also, and perhaps more important, often made one approach more natural than another; they led us to seek information in ways we might not have chosen without them.

How reliable is the interview material? What important sources of error are there in this kind of interview—where the interviewer comes from a completely different culture, perhaps with different systems of reference, and when the interviewer cannot speak the language of the respondent?

The interviews for this book were made during two long trips. They can be divided into two categories. One category consists of more or less official interviews with political leaders, people with government positions or in other official service, academics, etc. These were done in English, a language the respondents have mastered as well as or better than we have, and we nearly always used a tape recorder. These interviews are probably equivalent to interviews in our own country.

Other problems came up during village interviews, with

peasants ranging from farmworkers to landowners, with political cadres on the village level, etc. These interviews had to be done with interpreters, and only occasionally could the tape recorder be used to check on translations, misunderstandings, failures of memory, etc. One problem of interpreted interviews is, of course, that the interpreter can misinterpret questions and/or answers. He may have his own reasons for presenting a certain picture to the interviewer, and thus do his best to give the interviewer this picture—a thing which can occur more or less subconsciously.

Another and probably more significant problem with these interviews—a problem even with the English language interviews—is the often deep mistrust of the interviewer that the respondent feels. This is a problem which must be kept in mind when interpreting the official statistical information gathered by the census, interview analysis, etc. It is nearly impossible to come to an Indian village, with its oppression and absurdly unequal distribution of power, as an uncommitted observer who does not affect the situation by his own observation. Just asking a farmworker about his standard of living can change his life and the lives of others. Coming into an Indian village, full of great expectations and antagonisms, can mean fear in some huts and hope in others. Answers to the questions will be determined to a great extent by how the respondents regard the interviewer and the interpreter, what power they believe him to have, what they fear he is after, what they hope he can do for them. It must be more difficult to judge what a foreigner stands for—more than wealth and slightly undefinable power—than to judge the interpreter, who is ordinarily regarded as an official person connected with the authorities. The peasants will give answers which they think will cause the least difficulty for themselves. How can this be avoided? The interviewer can perhaps reduce the sources of error by choosing his interpreters with greatest care, by choosing someone whom the respondents will trust most—this implies that it is, for example, very difficult to interview more than one category of peasant in each village. The difficulty, of course, is finding such an interpreter. He must be known by the respondents in advance, must be trusted by the villagers and must speak English.

To get a grip on these problems, we tried various kinds of interpreters—people supplied by the Press Information Office, students, politicians from various parties, etc.—in the same areas, where we questioned peasants repeatedly about simple concrete facts like wages, wage systems, landowning, etc. It was apparent that the answers were as different as could be imagined and that they were always shaded in the directions one would expect. (This would surely be a worthwhile field for research.)

The interview material must therefore be treated with the greatest wariness and must be judged with the aid of all the background knowledge one has, in the same way that one judges the literature of this field, whose information was collected, after all, in the same way, with all the same sources of error.   Lasse and Lisa Berg

bibliography

This is not an exhaustive list of "books worth reading" about India, but rather a collection of books and articles that we found particularly interesting and that influenced the formulation of this book's chapters.

Politics

Alavi, Hamza. "Peasants and Revolution." In *Socialist Register 1965*. London: Merlin Press, 1965.

Chaudhuri, S. B. *Civil Disturbances during the British Rule in India (1765-1857)*. Calcutta: The World Press, 1955.

Gough, Kathleen. "Peasant Resistance and Revolt in South India." In *Pacific Affairs*, winter 1968-69.

Greene, Felix. *A Curtain of Ignorance*. London: Jonathan Cape, 1968.

Harrison, S. *India: The Most Dangerous Decades*. London: Oxford University Press, 1960.

Jones, W. H. M. *The Government and Politics of India*. London: Hutchinson University Library, 1964.

Lamb, Alastair. *The China-India Border*. London: Oxford University Press, 1964.

Moore, Barrington. *Social Origins of Democracy and Dictatorship*. Boston: Beacon Press, 1966.

Nehru, Jawaharlal. *Towards Freedom.* Boston: Beacon Press, 1958.

——. *The Discovery of India.* Bombay: Asia Publishing House, 1961.

Overstreet, G. D. and Windmiller, M. *Communism in India.* Berkeley and Los Angeles: University of California Press, 1959.

Segal, Ronald. *The Crisis of India.* London: Penguin, 1965.

The Sino-Indian Boundary Question. Peking: Foreign Languages Press, 1962.

Weiner, Myron. *Party Politics in India.* Princeton: Princeton University Press, 1957.

——. *The Politics of Scarcity.* Bombay: Asia Publishing House, 1963.

Economy
General

Bettelheim, C. *India Independent.* New York: Monthly Review Press, 1968.

Chand, Gyan. *Socialist Transformation of Indian Economy.* Bombay: Allied Publishers, 1965.

Chattopadhyay, B. "Marx and India's Crisis." In *Homage to Karl Marx*, edited by P. C. Joshi. New Delhi: People's Publishing House, 1969.

Myrdal, Gunnar. *Asian Drama.* New York: Pantheon, 1968.

Raj, K. N. *Indian Economic Growth.* Bombay: Allied Publishers, 1965.

——. *India, Pakistan, and China, Economic Growth and Outlook.* Bombay: Allied Publishers, 1967.

Rosen, George. *Democracy and Economic Change in India.* Bombay: Vora, 1966.

Roy, Ajit. *A Marxist Commentary on Economic Developments in India, 1951–1965.* Calcutta: National Publishers, 1967.

The Agricultural Economy

Datta, Bhupendra Nath. *Dialectics of Land-Economics of India*. Calcutta: Mohendra Publishing Committee, 1952.

Khusro, A. M. *Economic and Social Effects of Jagirdari Abolition and Land Reforms in Hyderabad*. Hyderabad: Osmania University Press, 1958.

Kotovsky, Grigory. *Agrarian Reforms in India*. New Delhi: People's Publishing House, 1962.

Ladejinsky, Wolf. "Green Revolution in Bihar." *Economic and Political Weekly* (Bombay), 27 September 1969.

Sen, Bhowani. *Evolution of Agrarian Relations in India*. New Delhi: People's Publishing House, 1962.

Thorner, Daniel and Alice. *Land and Labour in India*. Bombay: Asia Publishing House, 1962.

Foreign Aid, Investments, and Trade

Alavi, Hamza. "Imperialism, Old and New." In *Socialist Register 1964*. London: Merlin Press, 1964.

Eldridge, P. J. *The Politics of Foreign Aid in India*. London: Weidenfeld and Nicholson, 1969.

Kidron, Michael. *Foreign Investments in India*. London: Oxford University Press, 1965.

Roy, Ajit. *Economics and Politics of U.S. Foreign Aid*. Calcutta: National Publishers, 1966.

The Villages and the Caste System

Béteille, André. *Caste, Class, and Power*. Berkeley and Los Angeles: University of California Press, 1965.

Clinard, Marshall. *Slums and Community Development*. New York: The Free Press, 1966.

Dube, S. C. *Indian Village*. London: Routledge and Kegan Paul, 1955.

———. *India's Changing Villages*. London: Routledge and Kegan Paul, 1958.

Kosambi, D. D. *The Culture and Civilisation of Ancient India in Historical Outline*. London: Routledge and Kegan Paul, 1965.

Lewis, Oscar. *Village Life in Northern India*. New York: Random House, 1958.

Majumdar, D. N. *Caste and Communication in an Indian Village*. Bombay: Asia Publishing House, 1968.

Panikkar, K. M. *Asia and Western Dominance*. London: Hillary, 1959.

———. *A Survey of Indian History*. Bombay: Asia Publishing House, 1963.

Srinivas, M. N. *Caste in Modern India*. Bombay: Asia Publishing House, 1962.

———. *Social Change in Modern India*. Berkeley and Los Angeles: University of California Press, 1966.